Holidays In Cross-Stitch
1988

The Vanessa-Ann Collection

The Vanessa·Ann Collection Staff

Owners:
Terrece Beesley Woodruff
and Jo Packham
Executive Editor:
Margaret Shields Marti
Editor: Monica Smith
Art Director:
Trice Liljenquist Boerens
Needlework Director:
Nancy Whitley
Graphic Artist: Julie Truman
Graphing Director:
Susan Jorgensen
Operations Director:
Pamela Randall
Administrative Assistant:
Barbara Milburn
Customer Relations:
Kathi Allred

Designers

Trice Boerens
Linda Durbano
Margaret Marti
Jo Packham
Tina Richards
Doug Simmons
Julie Truman
Terrece Woodruff

This book is for you, Shirley, as a public thank-you for all the private love and support you have given us.

Your only daughter and her friends

© 1987 by Oxmoor House, Inc.
Book Division of Southern Progress Corporation
P.O. Box 2463, Birmingham, Alabama 35201

Library of Congress Catalog Number: 86-62285
ISBN: 0-8487-0713-3
ISSN: 0890-8230
Manufactured in the United States of America
First Printing 1987

Executive Editor: Candace N. Conard
Production Manager: Jerry Higdon
Associate Production Manager: Rick Litton
Art Director: Bob Nance

Holidays In Cross-Stitch 1988

Editor: Linda Baltzell Wright
Assistant Editor: Kim Eidson Crane
Editorial Assistant: Lenda Wyatt
Copy Chief: Mary Jean Haddin
Designer: Diana Smith Morrison
Photographers: Ryne Hazen, Howard L. Puckett,
   Colleen Duffley

The poems for Universal Children's Day
were written by Susan Jeppesen, Syracuse, Utah.

Much of the photography in this book was
done on location at Trends and Traditions,
part of Historic 25th Street in Ogden, Utah.
The Vanessa-Ann Collection expresses its
thanks to Mary Gaskill for her cooperation.

1 9 8 8
Contents

Introduction

Time passes so quickly! Another year is gone before you know it. But at The Vanessa-Ann Collection, we have found a way to slow it down. We capture it in cross-stitch—holiday by holiday!

Some holidays call for extensive plans and include the whole family. Others are celebrated with a small group of friends. And there are some special days, even very important ones, that go unnoticed except in our hearts. At Vanessa-Ann, we think almost any day can be made into a happy holiday.

Join us and needleworkers across the country in commemorating the most popular, the traditional, and the nearly unknown holidays. We hope that our fun and fanciful designs open up an exciting avenue for you and that your finished works are memorable measures of 1988. Happy stitching!

1988

JANUARY

S	M	T	W	T	F	S
					1	2
3	4	5	6	7	8	9
10	11	12	13	14	15	16
17	18	19	20	21	22	23
24	25	26	27	28	29	30
31						

FEBRUARY

S	M	T	W	T	F	S
	1	2	3	4	5	6
7	8	9	10	11	12	13
14	15	16	17	18	19	20
21	22	23	24	25	26	27
28	29					

MARCH

S	M	T	W	T	F	S
		1	2	3	4	5
6	7	8	9	10	11	12
13	14	15	16	17	18	19
20	21	22	23	24	25	26
27	28	29	30	31		

APRIL

S	M	T	W	T	F	S
					1	2
3	4	5	6	7	8	9
10	11	12	13	14	15	16
17	18	19	20	21	22	23
24	25	26	27	28	29	30

MAY

S	M	T	W	T	F	S
1	2	3	4	5	6	7
8	9	10	11	12	13	14
15	16	17	18	19	20	21
22	23	24	25	26	27	28
29	30	31				

JUNE

S	M	T	W	T	F	S
			1	2	3	4
5	6	7	8	9	10	11
12	13	14	15	16	17	18
19	20	21	22	23	24	25
26	27	28	29	30		

JULY

S	M	T	W	T	F	S
					1	2
3	4	5	6	7	8	9
10	11	12	13	14	15	16
17	18	19	20	21	22	23
24	25	26	27	28	29	30
31						

AUGUST

S	M	T	W	T	F	S
	1	2	3	4	5	6
7	8	9	10	11	12	13
14	15	16	17	18	19	20
21	22	23	24	25	26	27
28	29	30	31			

SEPTEMBER

S	M	T	W	T	F	S
				1	2	3
4	5	6	7	8	9	10
11	12	13	14	15	16	17
18	19	20	21	22	23	24
25	26	27	28	29	30	

OCTOBER

S	M	T	W	T	F	S
						1
2	3	4	5	6	7	8
9	10	11	12	13	14	15
16	17	18	19	20	21	22
23	24	25	26	27	28	29
30	31					

NOVEMBER

S	M	T	W	T	F	S
		1	2	3	4	5
6	7	8	9	10	11	12
13	14	15	16	17	18	19
20	21	22	23	24	25	26
27	28	29	30			

DECEMBER

S	M	T	W	T	F	S
				1	2	3
4	5	6	7	8	9	10
11	12	13	14	15	16	17
18	19	20	21	22	23	24
25	26	27	28	29	30	31

Kiss me I'm Irish

JANUARY 6
Three Kings Day

The visit of the Three Kings, or Wise Men, to Bethlehem is commemorated twelve days after Christmas. In medieval times Three Kings Day, or the Epiphany, marked the end of holiday activities. Today, in many parts of the world, this is a day of feasting, gift giving, and the last lighting of the Christmas lights.

Bearing Gifts

SAMPLE
Stitched on cream Hardanger 22 over two threads, the finished design size is 8⅜" x 9¼". The fabric was cut 15" x 16".

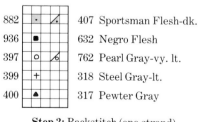

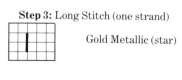

Bates			DMC (used for sample)
Step 1: Cross-stitch (three strands)			
1	·	⁄	White
778	–	⁄	754 Peach Flesh-lt.
306	▽		725 Topaz
47	✕		321 Christmas Red
44	●	⁄	816 Garnet
99		⁄	552 Violet-dk.
128	△		800 Delft-pale
130	∴		799 Delft-med.
132	□		797 Royal Blue
210	✕	⁄	562 Jade-med.
886	∴		677 Old Gold-vy. lt.
891	▫		676 Old Gold-lt.
307	∣	⁄	783 Christmas Gold
309	○	⁄	781 Topaz-dk.

882	·	⁄	407 Sportsman Flesh-dk.
936	■		632 Negro Flesh
397	○	⁄	762 Pearl Gray-vy. lt.
399	+		318 Steel Gray-lt.
400	▲		317 Pewter Gray

Step 2: Backstitch (one strand)

149		311 Navy Blue-med.

Step 3: Long Stitch (one strand)

	Gold Metallic (star)

FABRICS	DESIGN SIZES
Aida 11	8⅜" x 9¼"
Aida 14	6⅝" x 7¼"
Aida 18	5⅛" x 5⅝"
Hardanger 22	4⅛" x 4⅜"

Stitch Count: 92 x 102

JANUARY 23
National Pie Day

The pie is a gastronomical delight that sometimes approaches an art form. And few kinds of pie better represent this eating pleasure than America's favorite— the apple pie—saluted here.

Apple Pie

SAMPLE
Stitched on Linaida 14, the finished design size is 9⅜" x 7¼". The fabric was cut 16" x 14".

FABRICS	DESIGN SIZES
Aida 11	12" x 9¼"
Aida 14	9⅜" x 7¼"
Aida 18	7⅜" x 5⅝"
Hardanger 22	6" x 4⅝"

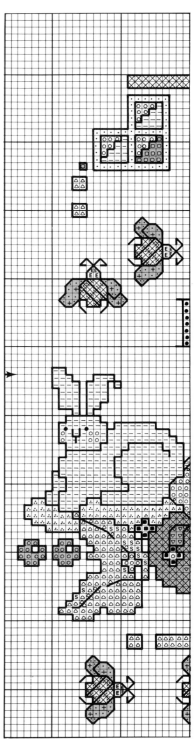

Stitch Count: 132 x 102

Bates		DMC (used for sample)
	Step 1: Cross-stitch (two strands)	
1	•	White
49	o ╱	963 Dusty Rose-vy. lt.
74	■	3354 Dusty Rose-lt.
69	▨ ╱	3687 Mauve
13	▽ ╱	347 Salmon-dk.
44	⊠ ╱	816 Garnet

95	554 Violet-lt.
159	3325 Baby Blue
978	322 Navy Blue-vy. lt.
149	336 Navy Blue
167	519 Sky Blue
168	807 Peacock Blue
215	368 Pistachio Green-lt.
216	367 Pistachio Green-dk.

246	319 Pistachio Green-vy. dk.
885	739 Tan-ultra vy. lt.
362	437 Tan-lt.
363	436 Tan
378	841 Beige Brown-lt.
379	840 Beige Brown-med.
400	414 Steel Gray-dk.
401	535 Ash Gray-vy. lt.

Step 2: Backstitch (one strand)

| 149 | 336 Navy Blue (lettering) |
| 382 | 3021 Brown Gray-dk. (all else) |

Step 3: French Knots (one strand)

| 382 | 3021 Brown Gray-dk. |

Valentine's Day

Sending homemade valentines became popular in the 1600s, but by the 1800s the new commercial cards were the custom of the day. This Valentine's Day, why not go back to that old-fashioned tradition with a cross-stitch greeting that says it all.

Wreath of Hearts

SAMPLES

The designs are stitched on white Aida 14. The fabric was cut 6" x 6" for each design. (A fabric with this stitch count must be used so that the design will fit the finished piece.)

Bates		DMC (used for sample)
Step 1: Cross-stitch (two strands)		
892		225 Shell Pink-vy. lt.
24		776 Pink-med.
59		326 Rose-vy. deep
43		815 Garnet-med.
158		747 Sky Blue-vy. lt.
Step 2: Backstitch (one strand)		
400		414 Steel Gray-dk.

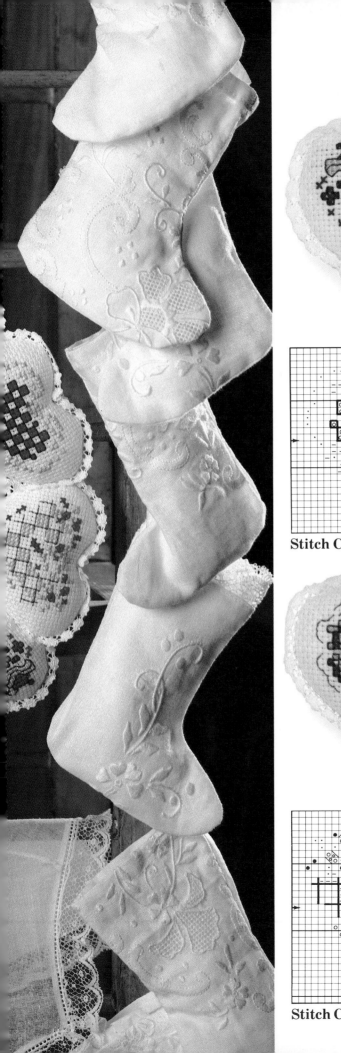

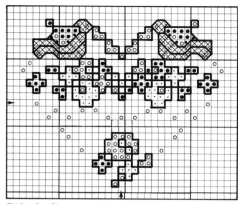

Stitch Count: 31 x 25

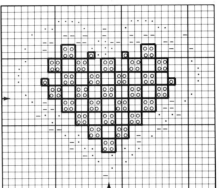

Stitch Count: 28 x 24

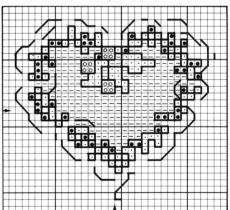

Stitch Count: 30 x 27

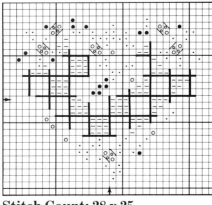

Stitch Count: 28 x 25

continued . . .

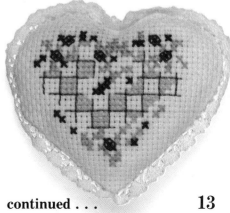

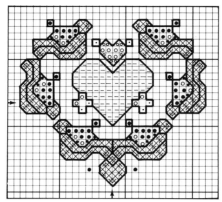

Stitch Count: 28 x 25

MATERIALS

Completed cross-stitch for nine
heart designs on white Aida 14
(three of which are the checkerboard pattern); matching thread
⅛ yard of 45"-wide white fabric
for heart backs
2½ yards of ¼"-wide white lace
with heart motif
7"-diameter wire ring (available
at craft stores)
Tracing paper for pattern
Dressmakers' pen
Stuffing
Optional hanger: 3 yards of ⅛"-
wide white satin ribbon

DIRECTIONS

All seams are ¼".

1. Trace the heart pattern and
cut out. Center the pattern over
each cross-stitch design and trace
with a dressmakers' pen. Cut out,
adding ¼" seam allowances.

2. On the right side of
the heart, with decorative
edge of the lace toward
the center, align straight
edge of lace with the pen
outline. Stitch to the
heart on this line.

3. From the white fabric, cut nine
hearts for the backs, adding ¼"
seam allowances. With right sides
together, match one front piece to
one back piece. Stitch the front
and back together, following the
previously sewn stitching line and
leaving a small opening. Clip the
curved edges and turn right side
out. Stuff lightly and slipstitch the
opening closed. Repeat for the remaining hearts.

4. With the edges of hearts
touching and the lace overlapping,
arrange the hearts in a circle (see
photo). Stitch the backs of the
hearts to the ring.

5. To make a hanger, cut the ribbon into four equal lengths. Tie the
ribbons to the ring behind the two
top hearts; then tie them into a
bow.

SAMPLE

Before stitching, piece the quilt
top, following Steps 3 and 4 of the
finishing instructions on page 17.
After the top is pieced, but before
the batting and backing are added,
stitch the designs. Refer to Diagram B and Key For Little Quilts
for design placement and color.

Heart: Stitched on muslin, using
Waste Canvas 14 over two sets of
threads, the finished design size is
2⅜" x 2¼". Cut the waste canvas
3½" x 3½".

FABRICS	DESIGN SIZES
Aida 11	1½" x 1½"
Aida 14	1¼" x 1⅛"
Aida 18	1" x ⅞"
Hardanger 22	¾" x ¾"

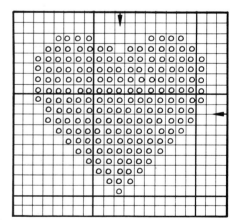

Stitch Count: 17 x 16

continued . . .

Heart Pattern

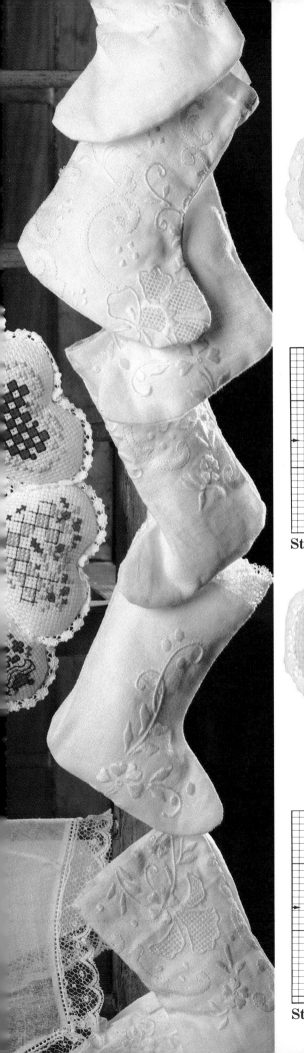

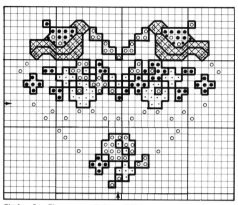

Stitch Count: 31 x 25

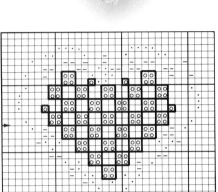

Stitch Count: 28 x 24

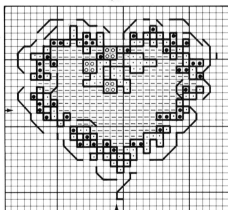

Stitch Count: 30 x 27

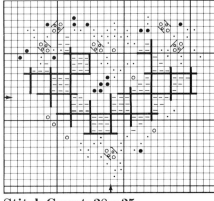

Stitch Count: 28 x 25

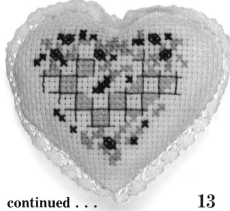

continued . . .

13

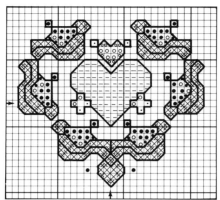

Stitch Count: 28 x 25

SAMPLE

Before stitching, piece the quilt top, following Steps 3 and 4 of the finishing instructions on page 17. After the top is pieced, but before the batting and backing are added, stitch the designs. Refer to Diagram B and Key For Little Quilts for design placement and color.

Heart: Stitched on muslin, using Waste Canvas 14 over two sets of threads, the finished design size is 2⅜" x 2¼". Cut the waste canvas 3½" x 3½".

FABRICS	DESIGN SIZES
Aida 11	1½" x 1½"
Aida 14	1¼" x 1⅛"
Aida 18	1" x ⅞"
Hardanger 22	¾" x ¾"

MATERIALS
Completed cross-stitch for nine heart designs on white Aida 14 (three of which are the checkerboard pattern); matching thread
⅛ yard of 45"-wide white fabric for heart backs
2½ yards of ¼"-wide white lace with heart motif
7"-diameter wire ring (available at craft stores)
Tracing paper for pattern
Dressmakers' pen
Stuffing
Optional hanger: 3 yards of ⅛"-wide white satin ribbon

DIRECTIONS
All seams are ¼".

1. Trace the heart pattern and cut out. Center the pattern over each cross-stitch design and trace with a dressmakers' pen. Cut out, adding ¼" seam allowances.

2. On the right side of the heart, with decorative edge of the lace toward the center, align straight edge of lace with the pen outline. Stitch to the heart on this line.

3. From the white fabric, cut nine hearts for the backs, adding ¼" seam allowances. With right sides together, match one front piece to one back piece. Stitch the front and back together, following the previously sewn stitching line and leaving a small opening. Clip the curved edges and turn right side out. Stuff lightly and slipstitch the opening closed. Repeat for the remaining hearts.

4. With the edges of hearts touching and the lace overlapping, arrange the hearts in a circle (see photo). Stitch the backs of the hearts to the ring.

5. To make a hanger, cut the ribbon into four equal lengths. Tie the ribbons to the ring behind the two top hearts; then tie them into a bow.

Heart Pattern

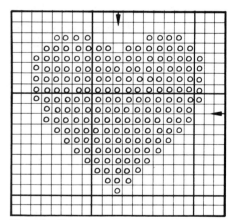

Stitch Count: 17 x 16

continued . . .

MATERIALS
Waste Canvas 14
1½ yards of unbleached muslin; matching thread
¼ yard of white muslin
20" x 26" piece of polyester batting
Dressmakers' pen
Paper for pattern

KEY FOR LITTLE QUILTS

Block 1: DMC 739. Couch the diagonal lines. Outline-stitch the edge of the motif. Quilt around the outside of motif with DMC White.

Block 2: DMC 738. Cross-stitch design; see sample information.

Block 3: DMC White. Satin-stitch the three small hearts. Outline-stitch the parallel lines above and below the hearts. Buttonhole-stitch around the edge of the motif. Quilt around the outside of the motif with DMC White.

Block 4: DMC 739. Make French knots, wrapped twice, around the edge of the motif.

Block 5: DMC 738. Quilt the outline of the motif and the inside heart.

Block 6: DMC White. Satin-stitch the small heart. Backstitch the remaining lines.

Block 7: DMC White. Stitch as desired, using buttonhole, back-stitch, chain, and herringbone stitches; see pattern.

Block 8: DMC White. Quilt the entire design.

Block 9: DMC White. Cross-stitch the entire design; see sample information.

Block 10: DMC 738. Herring-bone-stitch the three parallel lines. Outline-stitch the edge of the motif. Quilt around outside of motif with DMC White.

Block 11: DMC White. Cross-stitch the design; see the sample information.

Block 12: DMC 738. Repeat Block 5.

Block 13: DMC White. Quilt the design.

Block 14: DMC 739. Make lazy daisies for the flower petals. Make three French knots, wrapped twice, in the flower centers. Outline-stitch the solid line of the edge; see the pattern. Quilt the remainder of the edge of the motif with DMC White.

Block 15: DMC White. Repeat Block 1.

Block 16: DMC 739. Chain-stitch the design. Quilt around outside of motif.

Block 17: DMC White. Repeat Block 10.

Block 18: DMC 738. Cross-stitch the entire design; see the sample information.

Block 19: DMC White. Outline-stitch the motif. Quilt around outside of motif.

Block 20: DMC 738. Repeat Block 3.

Block 21: DMC 738. Quilt the entire design.

Block 22: DMC 739. Cross-stitch the entire design; see the sample information.

Block 23: DMC White. Repeat Block 1.

Block 24: DMC 738. Backstitch the letters.

Block 25: DMC White. Cross-stitch the entire design; see the sample information.

Block 26: DMC White. Chain-stitch the outline of the design.

Block 27: DMC 738. Repeat Block 3.

Block 28: DMC White. Repeat Block 14 but stitch lazy daisies on opposite side.

Block 29: DMC White. Cross-stitch the design; see the sample information.

Block 30: DMC 738. Repeat Block 5.

Block 31: DMC 739. Repeat Block 14.

Block 32: DMC White. Repeat Block 4.

Block 33: DMC White. Cross-stitch the design; see the sample information.

Block 34: DMC 739. Repeat Block 26.

Block 35: DMC 738. Repeat Block 7.

DIRECTIONS
All seams are ¼".

1. Before stitching the designs, piece the front of the quilt. Sew enough 3½"-wide strips of both the white and unbleached muslin to equal at least 50" of each. Stitch the two strips together on one long

Diagram B

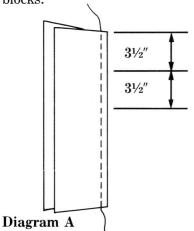

Diagram A

4. Mark the center of one long edge of each border strip and the center of each edge of the pieced top. With right sides together and centers matching, sew the border strips to the top. Stitch to within ¼″ of each corner; backstitch. Press seams toward the border.

5. To miter the corners, fold the right sides of two adjacent strips together and stitch at a 45-degree angle (Diagram C). Trim the seam allowance to ¼″ and press. Repeat for each corner.

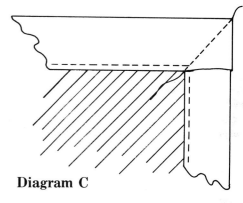

Diagram C

6. Baste the waste canvas onto the blocks that are to have cross-stitch designs. Complete the cross-stitch in the center of each designated block, using three strands of floss. Refer to Diagram B for placement and to the sample information for details. After stitching is complete, wet the fabric and remove the waste canvas (see General Instructions).

7. Make the pattern for the heart motif. Trace the pattern onto all the remaining blocks of the quilt top except the block with the message. Transfer all designs, referring to the patterns and Diagram B. Note that Block 28 is the reverse of Blocks 14 and 31. Complete all embroidery, using two strands (see the key).

edge. Cut into fourteen 3½″ segments (Diagram A). Then cut a 25″ strip of 3½″-wide unbleached muslin strips. Cut into seven 3½″ x 3½″ blocks.

2. From the unbleached muslin, cut one 19″ x 24″ piece for the quilt back and two 2½″ x 26″ and two 2½″ x 21″ strips for the border. Also cut 1½″-wide bias strips, piecing as needed, to equal 2¼ yards.

3. Arrange all blocks on a flat surface, using two sets of pieced pairs in each row, plus one additional unbleached muslin block. Refer to Diagram B for color placement. First stitch the blocks, right sides together, to form the horizontal rows. Then stitch the horizontal rows together, carefully matching seams. Press all seam allowances in the same direction.

continued . . .

8. Layer the quilt backing (wrong side up), the batting, and the quilt top (right side up) on a flat surface. Baste the layers together. Complete all quilted designs, using one strand of floss (see the key). Quilt the remainder by hand, using white floss. Quilt on all seam lines except the mitering at the corners.

9. With right sides together, stitch the binding to the quilt top, stopping ¼″ from the corner; back-stitch (Diagram D). Fold the bias at the corner at a right angle. Resume stitching with a backstitch ¼″ from the corner (Diagram E). Repeat at each corner.

Heart Pattern

YOU'VE STOLEN MY HEART

Block 24

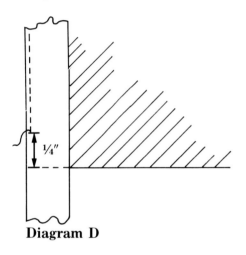

Diagram D

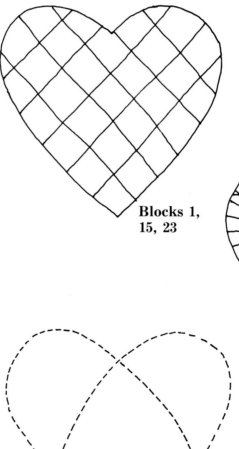

Blocks 1, 15, 23

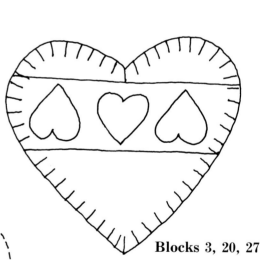

Blocks 3, 20, 27

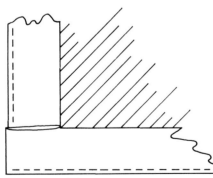

Diagram E

10. Fold edge of bias under ¼″ and then fold to wrong side of the quilt, making a ¼″-wide binding. Slip-stitch to the back, covering the stitching line and mitering each corner.

Blocks 5, 12, 30

18

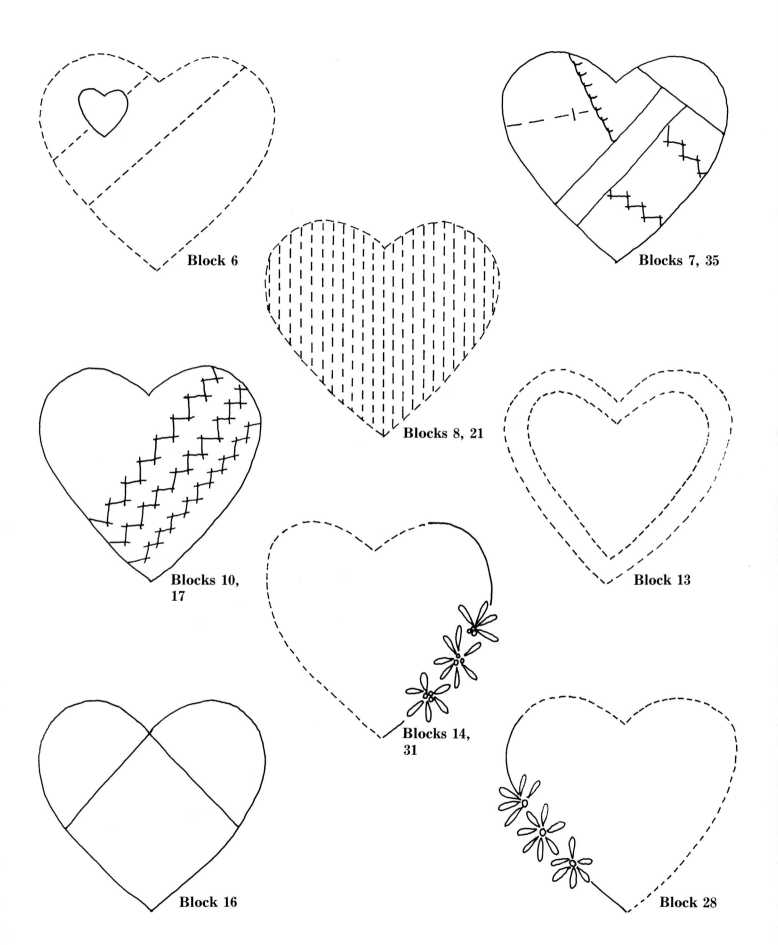

Block 6

Blocks 7, 35

Blocks 8, 21

Blocks 10, 17

Block 13

Blocks 14, 31

Block 16

Block 28

19

A Lover's Sampler

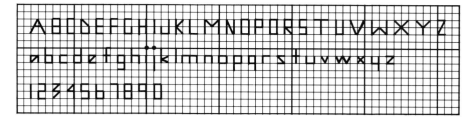

SAMPLE

Stitched on ash rose Lugana 25 over two threads, the finished design size is 5″ x 10⅜″. The fabric was cut 11″ x 16″. To personalize the sampler, transfer appropriate letters and numerals to graph paper and stitch in space indicated.

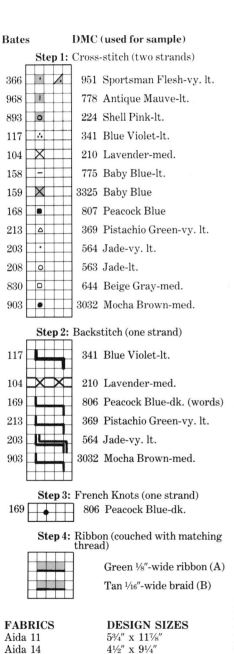

Bates		DMC (used for sample)	
Step 1: Cross-stitch (two strands)			
366		951	Sportsman Flesh-vy. lt.
968		778	Antique Mauve-lt.
893		224	Shell Pink-lt.
117		341	Blue Violet-lt.
104		210	Lavender-med.
158		775	Baby Blue-lt.
159		3325	Baby Blue
168		807	Peacock Blue
213		369	Pistachio Green-vy. lt.
203		564	Jade-vy. lt.
208		563	Jade-lt.
830		644	Beige Gray-med.
903		3032	Mocha Brown-med.

Bates		DMC	
Step 2: Backstitch (one strand)			
117		341	Blue Violet-lt.
104		210	Lavender-med.
169		806	Peacock Blue-dk. (words)
213		369	Pistachio Green-vy. lt.
203		564	Jade-vy. lt.
903		3032	Mocha Brown-med.

Step 3: French Knots (one strand)			
169		806	Peacock Blue-dk.

Step 4: Ribbon (couched with matching thread)

Green ⅛″-wide ribbon (A)

Tan 1/16″-wide braid (B)

FABRICS	DESIGN SIZES
Aida 11	5¾″ x 11⅞″
Aida 14	4½″ x 9¼″
Aida 18	3½″ x 7¼″
Hardanger 22	2⅞″ x 5⅞″

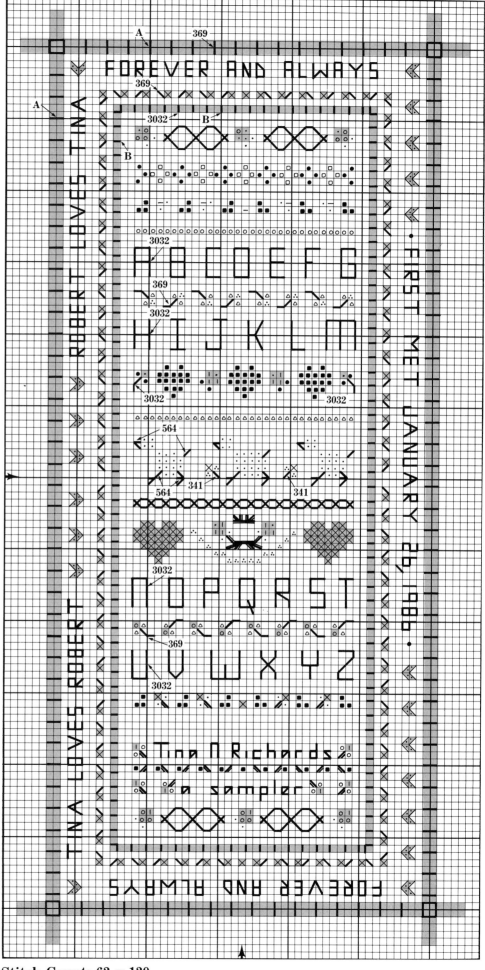

Stitch Count: 63 x 130

FEBRUARY 16
Mardi Gras

The words *Mardi Gras* literally mean Fat Tuesday. Since the Middle Ages, carnivals, spectacular parades, and masked balls have marked this holiday, which occurs the Tuesday before Ash Wednesday. This was the last chance for feasting and merrymaking before Lent (a period of fasting before Easter).

Carnival Time

SAMPLES

Carnival Mask: Stitched on white Belfast Linen 32 over two threads, the finished design size is 3″ x 3½″. The fabric was cut 9″ x 10″. Feathers were tacked in place with matching thread.

Stitch Count: 48 x 56

Bates			DMC (used for sample)
		Step 1: Cross-stitch (two strands)	
880	·	∕.	948 Peach Flesh-vy. lt.
778	–	∕	754 Peach Flesh-lt.
24	o	∕o	776 Pink-med.
27	X	∕X	899 Rose-med.
160	·	∕·	813 Blue-lt.
161	I	∕	826 Blue-med.
210		∕	562 Jade-med.
378	o	∕o	841 Beige Brown-lt.
380	∴		838 Beige Brown-vy. dk.

Step 2: Backstitch (one strand)

27	⌐_	899 Rose-med. (mouth, flowers)
378	⌐_	841 Beige Brown-lt. (nose)

Step 3: Beadwork

▲	Tangerine
●	Christmas Red
X	Light Blue
☐	Lilac
■	Iris
△	Light Green

FABRICS	**DESIGN SIZES**
Aida 11	4⅜" x 5⅛"
Aida 14	3⅜" x 4"
Aida 18	2⅝" x 3⅛"
Hardanger 22	2⅛" x 2½"

continued . . .

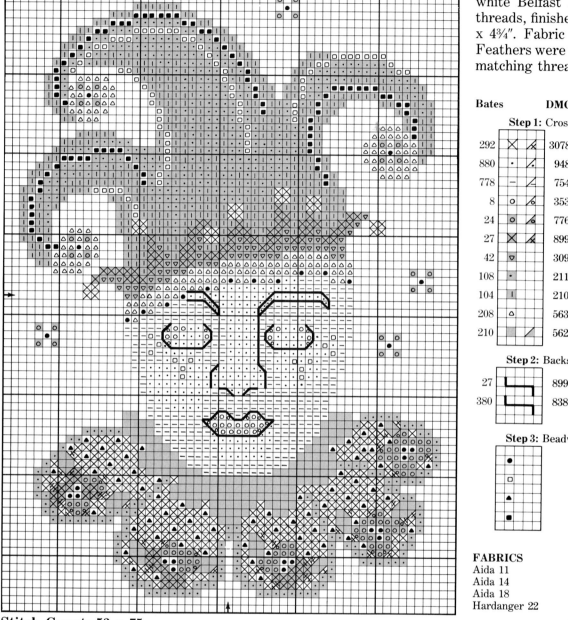

Stitch Count: 53 x 75

Mardi Gras Charade: Stitched on white Belfast Linen 32 over two threads, finished design size is 3⅜" x 4¾". Fabric was cut 10" x 11". Feathers were tacked in place with matching thread.

Bates			DMC	(used for sample)
Step 1: Cross-stitch (two strands)				
292	X	⧄	3078	Golden Yellow-vy. lt.
880	·	⧄	948	Peach Flesh-vy. lt.
778	–	⧄	754	Peach Flesh-lt.
8	o	⧄	353	Peach Flesh
24	o	⧄	776	Pink-med.
27	X	⧄	899	Rose-med.
42	▽		309	Rose-deep
108	·		211	Lavender-lt.
104	I		210	Lavender-med.
208	△		563	Jade-lt.
210		⧄	562	Jade-med.

Step 2: Backstitch (one strand)		
27	⌐	899 Rose-med. (mouth)
380	⌐	838 Beige Brown-vy. dk. (face)

Step 3: Beadwork

●	Christmas Red
□	Sapphire
▲	Light Green
■	Christmas Green

FABRICS	DESIGN SIZES
Aida 11	4¾" x 6⅞"
Aida 14	3¾" x 5⅜"
Aida 18	3" x 4⅛"
Hardanger 22	2⅜" x 3⅜"

The Jester

SAMPLE
Stitched on white Belfast Linen 32 over two threads, the finished design size is 5¼" x 9¼". The fabric was cut 12" x 16". Feathers were tacked in place with matching thread.

continued . . .

24

26

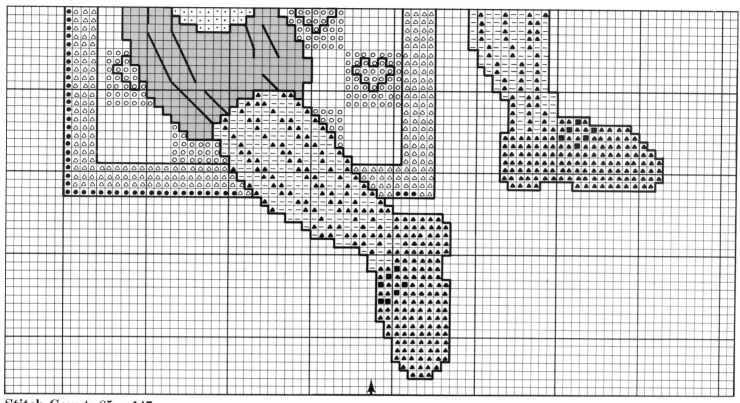

Stitch Count: 85 x 147

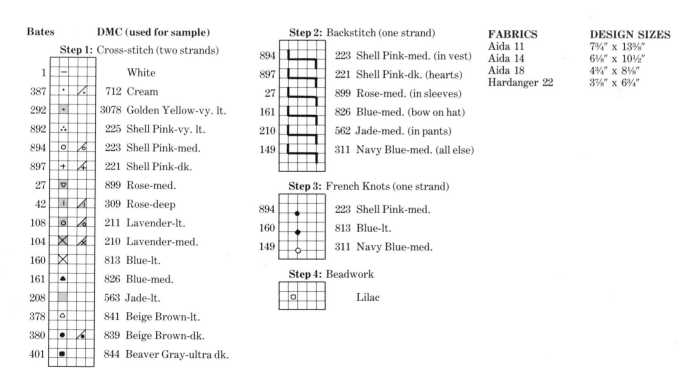

Bates		DMC (used for sample)
Step 1: Cross-stitch (two strands)		
1	–	White
387	· /	712 Cream
292	▪	3078 Golden Yellow-vy. lt.
892	∴	225 Shell Pink-vy. lt.
894	o /	223 Shell Pink-med.
897	+ ◢	221 Shell Pink-dk.
27	▽	899 Rose-med.
42	I /	309 Rose-deep
108	o ◢	211 Lavender-lt.
104	✕ ◢	210 Lavender-med.
160	✕	813 Blue-lt.
161	▲	826 Blue-med.
208		563 Jade-lt.
378	△	841 Beige Brown-lt.
380	● /	839 Beige Brown-dk.
401	■	844 Beaver Gray-ultra dk.

Bates		DMC (used for sample)
Step 2: Backstitch (one strand)		
894		223 Shell Pink-med. (in vest)
897		221 Shell Pink-dk. (hearts)
27		899 Rose-med. (in sleeves)
161		826 Blue-med. (bow on hat)
210		562 Jade-med. (in pants)
149		311 Navy Blue-med. (all else)

Bates		DMC (used for sample)
Step 3: French Knots (one strand)		
894	●	223 Shell Pink-med.
160	◆	813 Blue-lt.
149	○	311 Navy Blue-med.

Step 4: Beadwork		
	▢	Lilac

FABRICS
Aida 11
Aida 14
Aida 18
Hardanger 22

DESIGN SIZES
7¾" x 13⅜"
6⅛" x 10½"
4¾" x 8⅛"
3⅞" x 6¾"

FEBRUARY 17
Chinese New Year

To assure prosperity for the coming year, the Chinese New Year is celebrated by Chinese people all over the world. This year is the Year of the Dragon, a symbol of good luck.

The Dragon

SAMPLE
Stitched on light brown Linen 26 over two threads, the finished design size is 9⅞″ x 4⅞″. The fabric was cut 16″ x 11″.

MATERIALS
½ yard of 45″-wide tan chintz fabric
Professionally cut mat (see Step 1)
Glue
Masking tape
Pencil

continued . . .

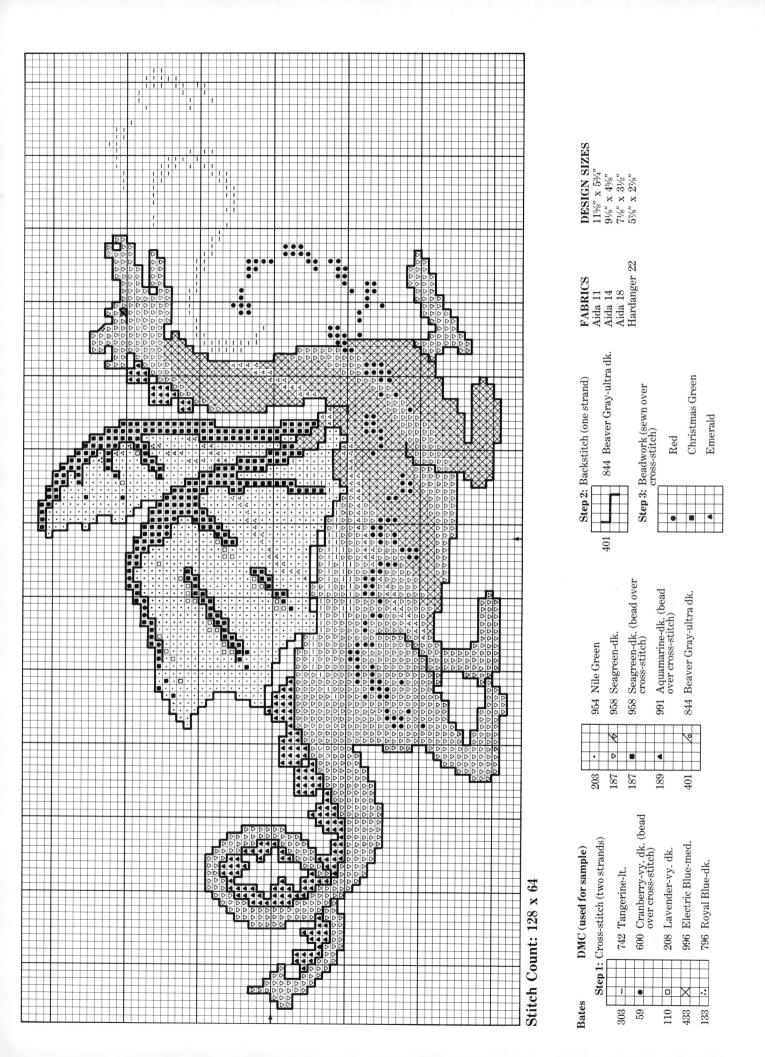

Stitch Count: 128 x 64

Bates		DMC (used for sample)

Step 1: Cross-stitch (two strands)

303	—	742	Tangerine-lt.
59	●	600	Cranberry-vy. dk. (bead over cross-stitch)
110	□	208	Lavender-vy. dk.
433	X	996	Electric Blue-med.
133	∴	796	Royal Blue-dk.

203	·	954	Nile Green
187	▷	958	Seagreen-dk.
187	■	958	Seagreen-dk. (bead over cross-stitch)
189	◀	991	Aquamarine-dk. (bead over cross-stitch)
401	◢	844	Beaver Gray-ultra dk.

Step 2: Backstitch (one strand)

| 401 | 844 | Beaver Gray-ultra dk. |

Step 3: Beadwork (sewn over cross-stitch)

●	Red
■	Christmas Green
▲	Emerald

FABRICS	DESIGN SIZES
Aida 11	11⅝" x 5¾"
Aida 14	9⅛" x 4⅝"
Aida 18	7⅛" x 3½"
Hardanger 22	5⅞" x 2⅞"

DIRECTIONS

1. To make sure the angles on your mat are square, have a professional framer cut the mat board. The outside edges are 17½″ x 15″. The inside edges are 11½″ x 9″.

2. To cover the mat, cut a 19½″ x 17″ piece from tan fabric. Cut six 3¼″ x 2½″ pieces for folded points.

3. Place the 19½″ x 17″ piece of fabric wrong side up on a flat surface. Center the mat on top of the fabric. Trace the inside edge, or window, of the mat. Make a second pencil line 2″ inside this line. Cut along this inside pencil line. Clip the corners to the window outline at a 45-degree angle.

4. Reposition the mat, aligning the window with the pencil line. Run a line of glue along the top edge of the window of the mat. Wrap the fabric around the mat and tape at two or three points. Repeat for window bottom and sides.

5. Run a line of glue along the top outside edge of the mat to within 2″ of the corners. Fold the fabric over the edge, making the surface taut. Tape. Repeat along the bottom edge; then the sides.

6. To make the points, fold two corners of one 3¼″ x 2½″ piece of fabric to the back, to form a point along the long edge. Repeat with the remaining pieces. Overlap the pieces so that the points are spaced evenly (see Diagram). Tape in place against the back of the mat.

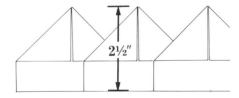

FEBRUARY 29
Bachelors' Day

Ladies, it's Leap Year and your turn to do the asking. Tradition has it that, during this year, women have the upper hand when it comes to asking for a date, or even proposing marriage. But there is one day during Leap Year when men are *not* fair game—Bachelors' Day. So put your ammunition away for the day and wait until tomorrow to go hunting.

Fair Game

SAMPLE
Stitched on white Aida 14, the finished design size is 4¼" x 5¾". The fabric was cut 7" x 9".

continued . . .

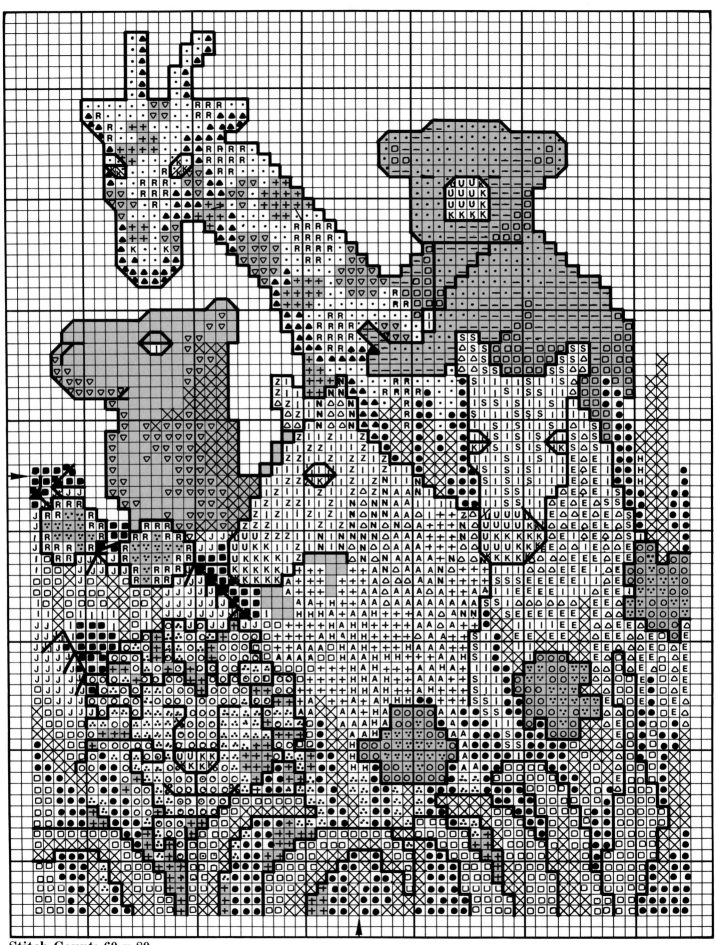

Stitch Count: 60 x 80

32

Bates			DMC (used for sample)

Step 1: Cross-stitch (two strands)

1	I	⁄	White
306	o	6	725 Topaz
303	∴	⁄	742 Tangerine-lt.
891	·	⁄	676 Old Gold-lt.
890	▲	◢	729 Old Gold-med.
901	R		680 Old Gold-dk.
307	+	⁄	783 Christmas Gold
66	o		3688 Mauve-med.
69	⋮		3687 Mauve
869	S		3042 Antique Violet-lt.
871	E		3041 Antique Violet-med.
920	Z	z	932 Antique Blue-lt.
921	N	⁄	931 Antique Blue-med.
265	□		3348 Yellow Green-lt.
266	X		3347 Yellow Green-med.
875	J	⁄	503 Blue Green-med.
876	●	◢	502 Blue Green
215	+		368 Pistachio Green-lt.
216	A		320 Pistachio Green-med.
246	H		319 Pistachio Green-vy. dk.
268	●	◢	3345 Hunter Green-dk.
362	▨		437 Tan-lt.
309	▽		435 Brown-vy. lt.
371	X		433 Brown-med.
378	·	⁄	841 Beige Brown-lt.
379	−	⁄	840 Beige Brown-med.
380	□		839 Beige Brown-dk.
397	△	◢	762 Pearl Gray-vy. lt.
399	U	⁄	318 Steel Gray-lt.
400	K	⁄	317 Pewter Gray

Step 2: Backstitch (one strand)

879		500 Blue Green-vy. dk. (stems)
382		3371 Black Brown (all else)

FABRICS

FABRICS	DESIGN SIZES
Aida 11	5½" x 7¼"
Aida 14	4¼" x 5¾"
Aida 18	3⅜" x 4½"
Hardanger 22	2¾" x 3⅝"

MATERIALS

Completed cross-stitch on white Aida 14; matching thread

One 6¾" x 8½" piece of mat board
One 8" x 10" piece of green fabric; matching thread
One 5½" x 1½" piece of muslin
1½ yards of ⅛"-wide green satin ribbon
Two 4½" pieces of heavy cording
Fusible webbing
White glue
Zipper foot

DIRECTIONS

1. Cut the Aida 5½" x 8", with the design centered horizontally and positioned 1¼" above the lower edge.

2. Place the muslin behind the unstitched area below the design. Sew the two fabrics together, stitching below and as close as possible to the design. Between the Aida and the muslin, place one piece of cording against the stitching line. Keep the muslin smooth and shape the Aida over the cording. Stitch close to cording, using a zipper foot. Repeat with second piece of cording, placing it close to first. Trim Aida to 5¼" x 7", with design centered.

3. Cut the green fabric into two 2" x 10" strips and two 2" x 8" strips. Mark the center of one long edge on each strip. Also mark the center of each edge of the Aida. Match the centers of the long strips to the long edges and short strips to the short edges of the Aida. Stitch with a ¼" seam to within ¼" of each corner; backstitch.

4. To miter the corners, fold the right sides of two adjacent strips together and stitch at a 45-degree angle. Trim the seam allowance to ¼". Repeat for each corner.

5. Trim the piece to measure 6¾" x 8½" with the design centered. Cut the fusible webbing 6¾" x 8½". Fuse the piece to the mat board.

6. Cut an 18" length of ribbon. Fold the remaining ribbon into two 3" loops with loose ends. Tie the 18" length around the center of the loops. Glue the bow between the lines of cording.

MARCH 11
Johnny Appleseed Day

John Chapman, better known as Johnny Appleseed, was born in 1774 and died on this day in 1847. He spent his adult life planting orchards, and selling and giving away apple seedlings across the American Midwest. Imagine him in his tin cooking-pot hat and coffee-sack tunic, strolling barefoot through this cross-stitched orchard. A perfect companion piece to this design is The Pumpkin Harvest, celebrating national Pumpkin Day.

The Apple Orchard

SAMPLE
Stitched on yellow Canvas 22 over two threads, the finished design size is 12¾" x 10⅛". The fabric was cut 19" x 17".

continued . . .

Bates | | DMC (used for sample)

Step 1: Cross-stitch (three strands)

288			445	Lemon-lt.
50	U		605	Cranberry-vy. lt.
10	+		352	Coral-lt.
35			891	Carnation-dk.
46	ɛ		666	Christmas Red-bright
44	●		816	Garnet
265	·		3348	Yellow Green-lt.
266	s		471	Avocado Green-vy. lt.
239	I		702	Kelly Green
205	✕		911	Emerald Green-med.
256			906	Parrot Green-med.
258	o		904	Parrot Green-vy. dk.
246	✕		986	Forest Green-vy. dk.
879	■		890	Pistachio Green-ultra dk.
349	+		921	Copper
339	o		920	Copper-med.
363	–		436	Tan
376	·		842	Beige Brown-vy. lt.
378	□		841	Beige Brown-lt.
379	▽		840	Beige Brown-med.
357	H		801	Coffee Brown-dk.
400	▲		317	Pewter Gray

Step 2: Backstitch (two strands)

| 339 | ⌐ | 920 | Copper-med. (matches trunk) |
| 363 | ⌐ | 436 | Tan (matches trunk) |

Step 3: Beadwork

N	Yellow
△	Pink
□	Garnet

FABRICS   **DESIGN SIZES**
Aida 11   12¾" x 10⅛"
Aida 14   10" x 8"
Aida 18   7¾" x 6¼"
Hardanger 22   6¼" x 5⅛"

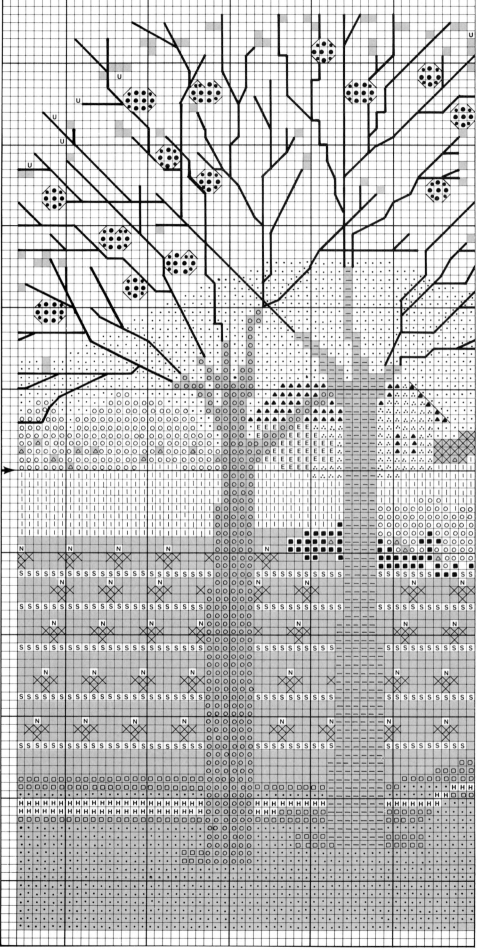

Stitch Count: 140 x 112

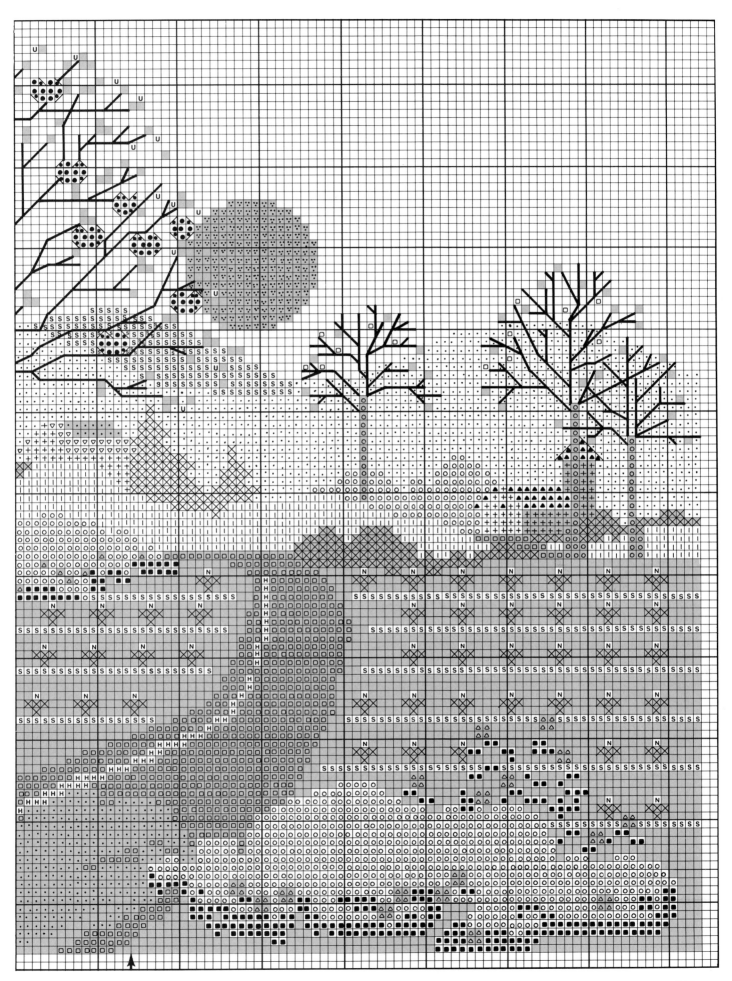

MARCH 17
St. Patrick's Day

Ireland's patron saint, for whom this holiday is named, lived during the fourth century. In his extensive travels he used the three-leafed clover to explain the Holy Trinity to the people. Today Irish (and not-so-Irish) people the world over make merry on St. Patrick's Day by wearing a shamrock.

An Irish Bib

SAMPLE
Stitched on white Aida 14, the finished design size is 4¼" x 2⅝". The fabric was cut 11" x 8".

Bates		DMC (used for sample)
Step 1: Cross-stitch (two strands)		
42	·	335 Rose
167	●	598 Turquoise-lt.
214	○	966 Baby Green-med.
205	✕	911 Emerald Green-med.
923	■	699 Christmas Green
Step 2: Backstitch (one strand)		
59		326 Rose-vy. deep

FABRICS	DESIGN SIZES
Aida 11	5⅜" x 3¼"
Aida 18	3¼" x 2"
Hardanger 22	2⅝" x 1⅝"

Stitch Count: 59 x 36

Place on fold.

MATERIALS

Completed cross-stitch on white Aida 14
9½″ x 6½″ piece of unstitched white Aida 14 for back
¼ yard of 45″-wide green satin fabric; matching thread
9½″ x 6½″ piece of fusing material
Tracing paper for pattern
Dressmakers' pen

DIRECTIONS

1. Trace the bib pattern and cut out. Place the pattern on the stitched Aida, with the design centered horizontally and positioned 2″ from the bottom of the pattern. Cut out the bib front.

2. Cut one bib piece for the back from the unstitched Aida and one from the fusing material.

3. From the satin fabric, cut a 1″-wide bias strip, piecing as needed to equal 1¼ yards. Cut a second 1″-wide bias strip 20″ long.

4. Sandwich the fusing material between the unstitched Aida and the stitched Aida, with stitched design facing out. Fuse together.

5. With right sides together, machine-stitch bias strip along sides and bottom of bib front. Press under ¼″ of opposite edge of bias. Fold to the back and slipstitch.

6. Mark centers of the 1¼-yard bias strip and top edge of bib. Match center marks and machine-stitch bias strip to front of bib. Press under ¼″ of opposite edge of bias strip, and then fold to the back. Slipstitch in place.

7. To finish the ties, fold ¼″ to the inside along both long edges and press. Stitch together by hand or machine. Knot tie ends.

International Children's Book Day

Once upon a time, she learned her ABCs, and a wonderland of fairy tales and adventures unfolded before her. Hans Christian Andersen, the author of more than 150 fairy tales including the classic *The Ugly Duckling,* was born on April 2, 1805. So it's fitting that we celebrate the world of children's literature on this day.

ABC Blocks

SAMPLES: Fabric with a stitch count of 14 must be used so that the designs will fit the blocks.

ABC Blocks: Stitched on Aida 14: Block A—yellow, Block B—green, Block C—pink. The finished design sizes are 3¼″ x 3¼″. The fabrics were cut 6″ x 6″.

Block A

Bates		DMC (used for sample)	
Step 1: Cross-stitch (two strands)			
886	·	677	Old Gold-vy. lt.
893	△	224	Shell Pink-lt.
869	✕	3042	Antique Violet-lt.
159	○	3325	Baby Blue
203	▫	564	Jade-vy. lt.
186	●	993	Aquamarine-lt.
162	▪	825	Blue-dk.
Step 2: Backstitch (one strand)			
162		825	Blue-dk.

Block B

Bates		DMC (used for sample)	
Step 1: Cross-stitch (two strands)			
886	·	677	Old Gold-vy. lt.
893	△	224	Shell Pink
869	✕	3042	Antique Violet-lt.
110	∴	208	Lavender-vy. dk.
159	○	3325	Baby Blue
203	▫	564	Jade-vy. lt.
Step 2: Backstitch (one strand)			
110		208	Lavender-vy. dk. (around Lavender areas)
162		825	Blue-dk. (all else)

Block C

Bates		DMC (used for sample)	
Step 1: Cross-stitch (two strands)			
886	·	677	Old Gold-vy. lt.
893	△	224	Shell Pink-lt.
869	✕ ⁄	3042	Antique Violet-lt.
159	○ ⁄	3325	Baby Blue
203	▫	564	Jade-vy. lt.
186	●	993	Aquamarine-lt.
Step 2: Backstitch (one strand)			
878		501	Blue Green-dk.

Block A Stitch Count: 45 x 45

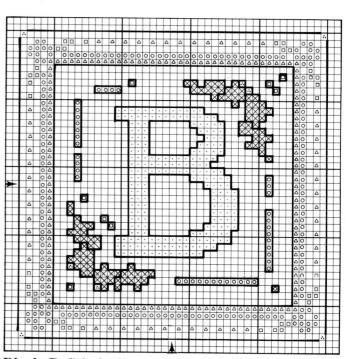

Block B Stitch Count: 45 x 45

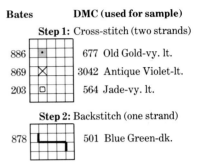

Flowers in Squares: Stitched on pink Aida 14, the finished design size is 3¼" x 3¼". The fabric was cut 6" x 6".

Bates		DMC (used for sample)
Step 1: Cross-stitch (two strands)		
886		677 Old Gold-vy. lt.
869		3042 Antique Violet-lt.
203		564 Jade-vy. lt.
Step 2: Backstitch (one strand)		
878		501 Blue Green-dk.

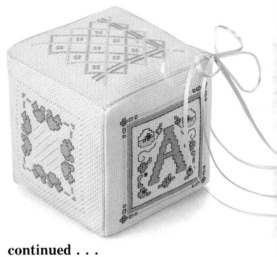

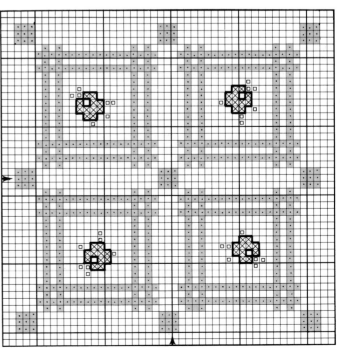

continued . . .

Block C Stitch Count: 45 x 45

Flowers in Squares Stitch Count: 45 x 45

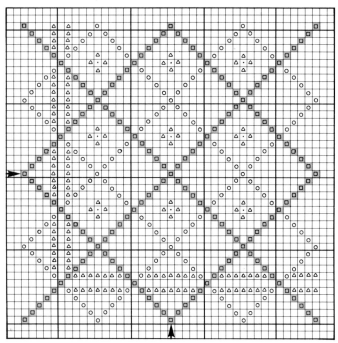

Diamonds Stitch Count: 41 x 41

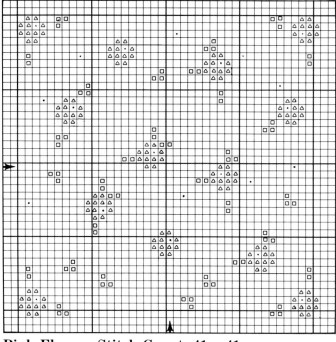

Pink Flowers Stitch Count: 41 x 41

Diamonds: Stitched on yellow or pink Aida 14, the finished design size is 2⅞″ x 2⅞″. The fabric was cut 6″ x 6″.

Blue Birds: Stitched on green Aida 14, the finished design size is 2⅞″ x 2⅞″. Fabric was cut 6″ x 6″.

Flower Baskets: Stitched on green Aida 14, the finished design size is 2⅞″ x 2⅞″. The fabric was cut 6″ x 6″.

Bates		DMC (used for sample)
	Step 1: Cross-stitch (two strands)	
886	·	677 Old Gold-vy. lt.
893	△	224 Shell Pink-lt.
159	o	3325 Baby Blue
203	▣	564 Jade-vy. lt.

Bates		DMC (used for sample)
	Step 1: Cross-stitch (two strands)	
886	·	677 Old Gold-vy. lt.
893	△	224 Shell Pink-lt.
869	✕	3042 Antique Violet-lt.
159	o /	3325 Baby Blue
	Step 2: Backstitch (one strand)	
162		825 Blue-dk.

Bates		DMC (used for sample)
	Step 1: Cross-stitch (two strands)	
886	·	677 Old Gold-vy. lt.
869	✕	3042 Antique Violet-lt.
159	o	3325 Baby Blue
203	▣	564 Jade-vy. lt.
186	●	993 Aquamarine-lt.
	Step 2: Backstitch (one strand)	
878		501 Blue Green-dk.

Pink Flowers: Stitched on yellow Aida 14, the finished design size is 2⅞″ x 2⅞″. Fabric was cut 6″ x 6″.

Bates		DMC (used for sample)
	Step 1: Cross-stitch (two strands)	
886	·	677 Old Gold-vy. lt.
893	△	224 Shell Pink-lt.
203	▣	564 Jade-vy. lt.

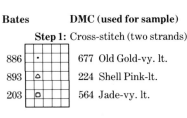

MATERIALS (for three blocks)
Four completed cross-stitch designs on each color—yellow, pink, and green Aida 14; matching thread
Unstitched yellow, pink, and green Aida 14

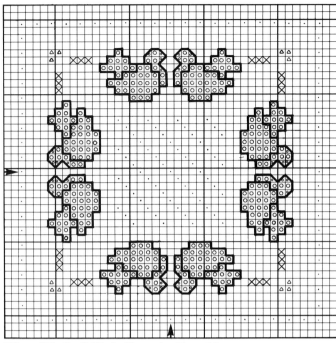

Blue Birds Stitch Count: 41 x 41

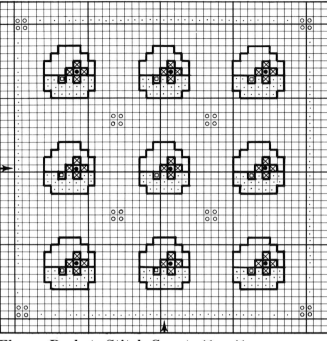

Flower Baskets Stitch Count: 41 x 41

3 yards of ⅛"-wide white satin ribbon
3 yards of ⅛"-wide green or pink satin ribbon; matching thread
12" x 8" x 2" foam pillow form
Polyester batting
Glue

DIRECTIONS
All seam allowances are ½".

1. From each color of Aida, cut six 5" squares. Be sure designs are centered on stitched squares.

2. Cut the pillow form into six 4" x 4" x 2" pieces. Stack and glue together in pairs. From the batting, cut 4"-wide strips. Cover each foam cube with one layer of batting. Loosely baste the batting to the cube.

3. With right sides together, stitch one side of a plain Aida square to a design square. Stitch an additional Aida square to both

of these squares, making a strip of four (see Diagram).

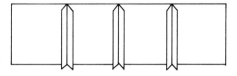

4. Stitch the right sides of the two free ends of the strip together, making a tube.

5. With right sides together, place the fifth Aida piece on top of the side panel, matching the corners to the side seams of one of the squares in the strip. Stitch, beginning in one corner and stitching to, but not through, the next side seam; backstitch. Stitch each of the remaining three sides of the square to the side panel in the same manner.

6. With right sides together, stitch one side of the remaining Aida square to the other end of the

block. Sew between the seams and backstitch.

7. Turn the Aida right side out and insert the foam block. Fold the partially attached square over the foam, matching the corners to the side seams. Turn under a ½" seam allowance and slipstitch the remaining three sides closed.

8. Cut ribbon into one-yard lengths. Handling two ribbon lengths as one unit, tie a bow and tack it to upper right corner of front of block.

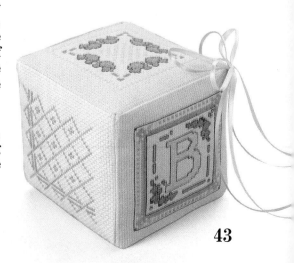

APRIL 3
Easter

Regardless of where spring's arrival is marked on the calendar, Easter is the real introduction to the season. Mark this, the most important holiday of the Christian calendar, with cross-stitched eggs inspired by Amish designs, or our other new projects with an Easter theme.

Geometric Easter Eggs

SAMPLES
Stitched on white Linda 27 over two threads, the finished design size of each is 1⅞" x 2⅝". The fabric was cut 6" x 7".

MATERIALS (for one egg)
Completed cross-stitch on white Linda 27
5" x 6" piece of print fabric for back
⅝ yard of ¼"-wide white lace
3½" Styrofoam egg
Dull paring knife for scoring
Glue

DIRECTIONS
1. Cut the Linda 5" x 6", with the design centered.

2. Score the vertical center of the egg.

continued . . .

45

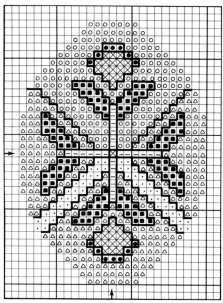

Design 1

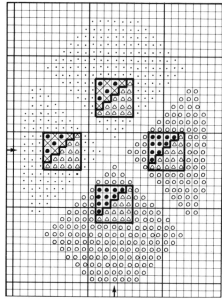

Design 2

Design 3

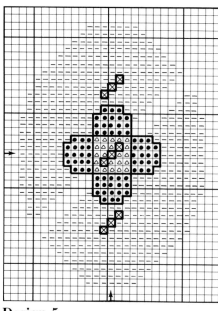

Design 4

Design 5

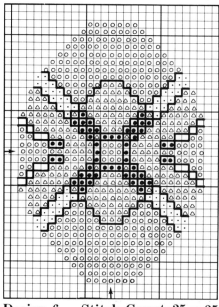

Design 6   Stitch Count: 25 x 35

3. Center print fabric over the back of the egg and tuck it into scored line. Trim extending fabric edges close to egg. Place the Linda over the front of the egg with the design centered. Tuck fabric into scored line and trim.

4. Beginning 3″ to 5″ from the end of the lace and at the lower right side of the egg, glue the lace over the scored line. Tie a bow or knot near the bottom of the egg. Trim the ends.

Bates		DMC (used for sample)
		Step 1: Cross-stitch (two strands)
891	·	676 Old Gold-lt.
42	X	3350 Dusty Rose-vy. dk.
99	●	552 Violet-dk.
167	○	519 Sky Blue
168	△	518 Wedgewood-lt.
203	–	564 Jade-vy. lt.
187	■	958 Seagreen-dk.

Step 2: Backstitch (one strand)

72		902 Garnet-vy. dk. (Designs 1 and 3)
149		311 Navy Blue-med. (Designs 2, 4, 5, 6)

FABRICS	DESIGN SIZES
Aida 11	2¼″ x 3⅛″
Aida 14	1¾″ x 2½″
Aida 18	1⅜″ x 2″
Hardanger 22	1⅛″ x 1⅝″

46

Jesus and the Children

SAMPLE
Stitched on white Belfast Linen 32, picture and verse are stitched on separate pieces of fabric.

Picture: Finished design size is 9⅝" x 12¼". Fabric was cut 16" x 19".
continued . . .

Top left quarter of design

Top right quarter of design

continued . . .

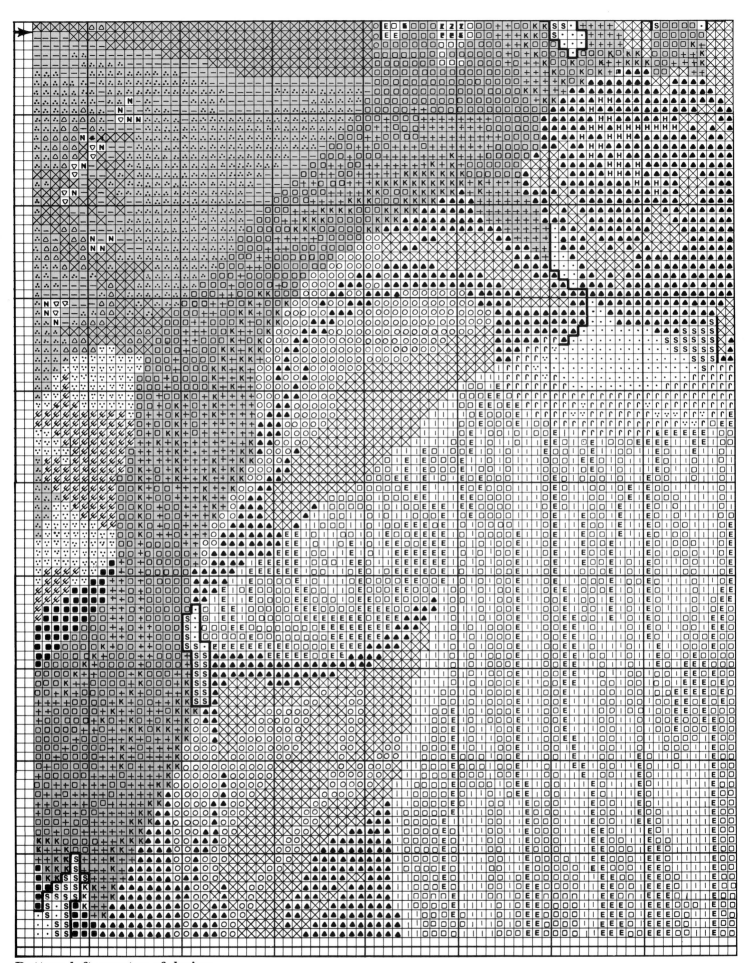

Bottom left quarter of design

50

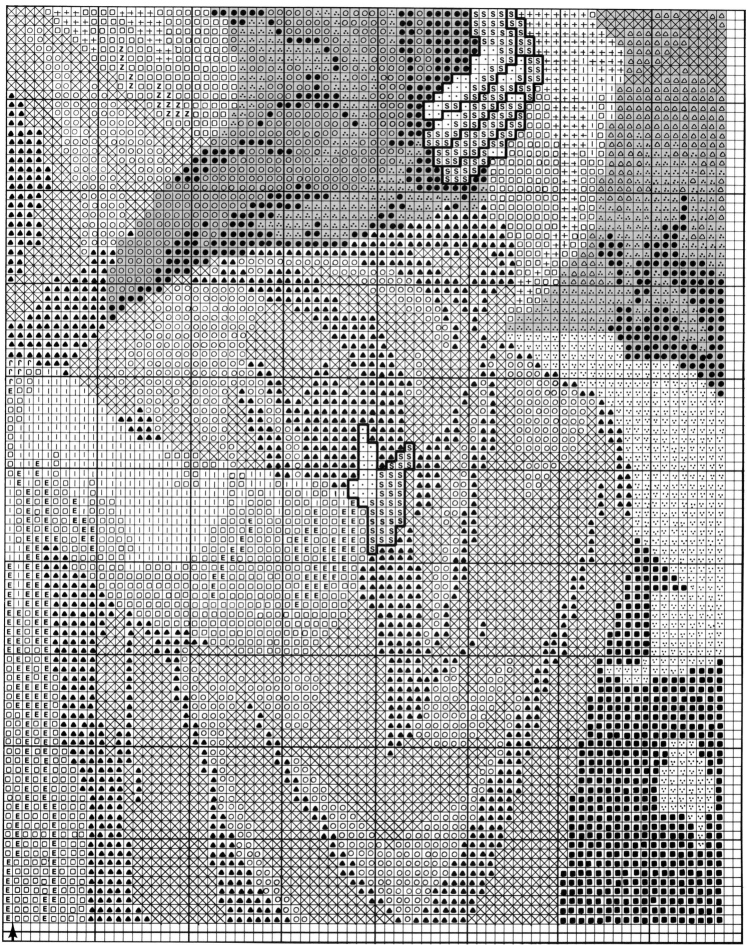

Bottom right quarter of design

Bates		DMC (used for sample)
Step 1: Cross-stitch (two strands)		
1	┌	White
386	+	746 Off White
300	Z	745 Yellow-lt. pale
778	· /	754 Peach Flesh-lt.
868	S ⧄	758 Terra Cotta-lt.
882	R	407 Sportsman Flesh-dk.
8	U	761 Salmon-lt.
26	N ⧄	957 Geranium-pale
59	▽ ⧄	326 Rose-vy. deep
159	▢	827 Blue-vy. lt.
920	+	932 Antique Blue-lt.
921	K ⧄	931 Antique Blue-med.
265	−	3348 Yellow Green-lt.
266	△	3347 Yellow Green-med.
268	✕	3345 Hunter Green-dk.
215	○	368 Pistachio Green-lt.
216	∴	367 Pistachio Green-dk.
879	●	890 Pistachio Green-ultra dk.
891	I	676 Old Gold-lt.
890	▢	729 Old Gold-med.
375	E ⧄	420 Hazel Nut Brown-dk.
363	○	436 Tan
370	✕	434 Brown-lt.
357	▲	801 Coffee Brown-dk.
382	H	3371 Black Brown
398	⋮	415 Pearl Gray
400	⧄	414 Steel Gray-dk.
401	■	413 Pewter Gray-dk.

Step 2: Filet Cross-stitch (one strand)

1	·	White
159	▨	827 Blue-vy. lt.

Step 3: Backstitch (one strand)

26		957 Geranium-pale (girl's mouth)
59		326 Rose-vy. deep (boy's mouth)
879		890 Pistachio Green-ultra dk. (tree, lettering)
375		420 Hazel Nut Brown-dk. (eyebrows, boy's nose)
357		801 Coffee Brown-dk. (all else)

FABRICS	DESIGN SIZES
Aida 11	14″ x 17⅝″
Aida 14	11″ x 14″
Aida 18	8½″ x 11″
Hardanger 22	7″ x 9″

Verse: The finished design size is 9¾″ x 2¼″. Fabric was cut 16″ x 9″.

FABRICS	DESIGN SIZES
Aida 11	14⅞″ x 3⅜″
Aida 14	11″ x 2⅝″
Aida 18	8⅝″ x 2″
Hardanger 22	7″ x 1⅝″

Stitch Count: 155 x 37

My Tulips Are Yours

SAMPLE

Before stitching, piece the quilt top, following Steps 3 and 4 of the finishing instructions on page 17. After the top is pieced, but before the batting and backing are added, stitch the designs. Refer to Diagram B and Key for Little Quilts for design placement and color.

Tulips: Stitched on muslin, using Waste Canvas 14 over two sets of threads, the finished design size is 2¼" x 2⅜". Cut the waste canvas 3½" x 3½".

FABRICS	DESIGN SIZES
Aida 11	1½" x 1½"
Aida 14	1⅛" x 1¼"
Aida 18	⅞" x 1"
Hardanger 22	¾" x ¾"

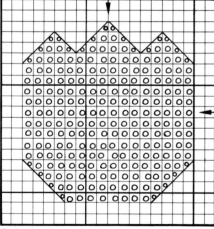

Stitch Count: 16 x 17

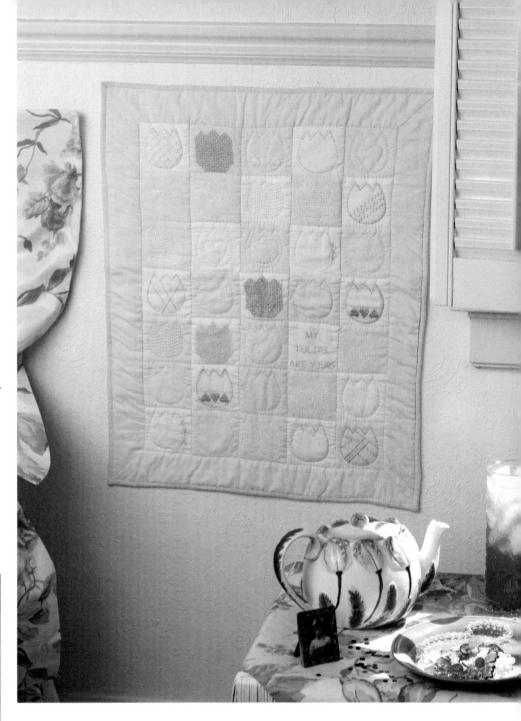

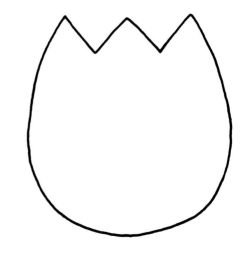

MY
TULIPS
ARE YOURS

An Easter Celebration

SAMPLE

Stitched on white Linda 27 over two threads, the finished design size is 8⅛" x 9". The fabric was cut 15" x 15".

FABRICS	DESIGN SIZES
Aida 11	9⅞" x 11⅛"
Aida 14	7¾" x 8¾"
Aida 18	6" x 6¾"
Hardanger 22	5" x 5½"

Bates		DMC (used for sample)
Step 1: Cross-stitch (two strands)		
295	·	726 Topaz-lt.
303	–	742 Tangerine-lt.
778	ı	948 Peach Flesh-vy. lt.
328	▽	3341 Apricot
333	▫	608 Orange Red
75	·	604 Cranberry-lt.
76	△	603 Cranberry
78	✕	601 Cranberry-dk.
118		340 Blue Violet-med.
119	◦	333 Blue Violet-dk.
186	▫	959 Seagreen-med.

Bates		DMC (used for sample)
187	●	958 Seagreen-dk.
209	○	913 Nile Green-med.
228	■	910 Emerald Green-dk.
309	∴	435 Brown-vy. lt.
371	✕	433 Brown-med.
403	▲	310 Black

Step 2: Backstitch (one strand)

403	⌐	310 Black

Step 3: Long Stitch (one strand)

Black pearl cotton #8

Black pearl cotton #8

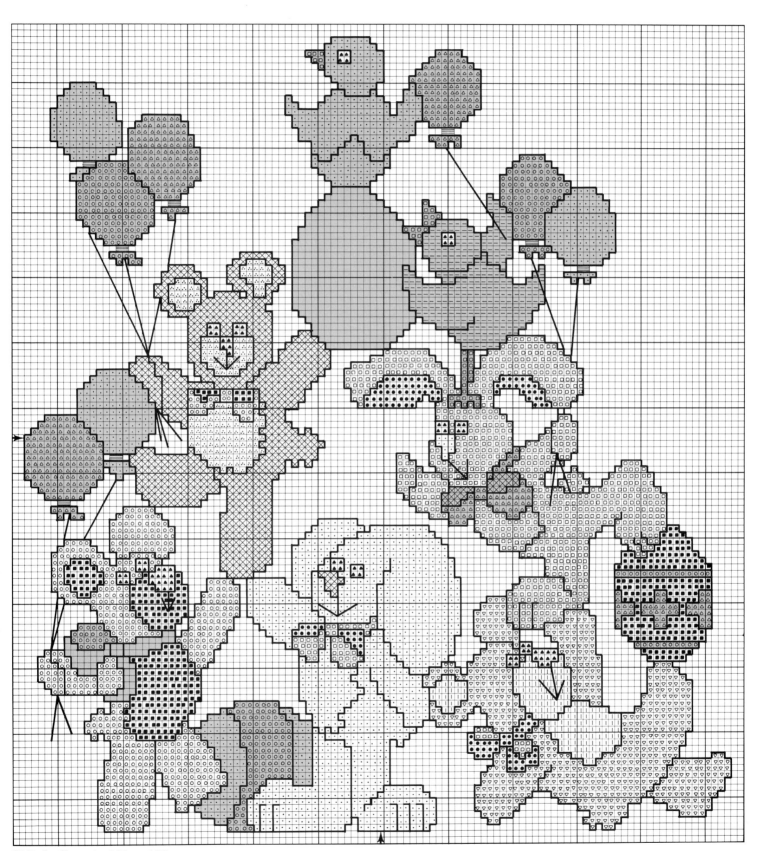

Stitch Count: 109 x 122

55

MAY 1
May Day Spring Pillow

Spring is in the air! Flowers are blooming, and birds are singing. It must be May! May Day is a worldwide festival that originated with the Romans, who offered flowers to Flora, their goddess of spring. *Our* springtime offering is a new pillow to decorate your home.

SAMPLE
Stitched on white Linda 27 over two threads, the finished design size is 4⅛" x 3½". The fabric was cut 8" x 8".

FABRICS	DESIGN SIZES
Aida 11	5⅞" x 5⅛"
Aida 14	4⅝" x 4⅛"
Aida 18	3⅝" x 3⅛"
Hardanger 22	3" x 2⅝"

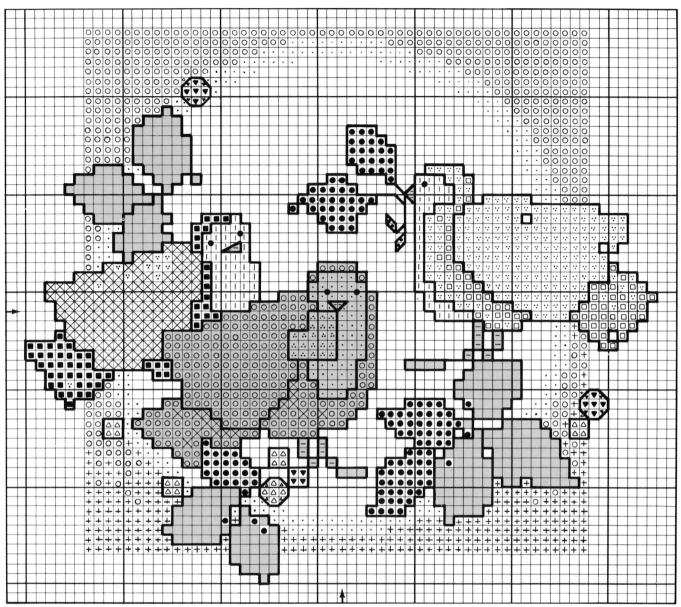

Stitch Count: 65 x 57

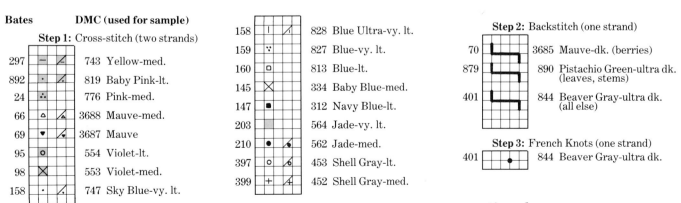

Bates		DMC (used for sample)

Step 1: Cross-stitch (two strands)

297		743 Yellow-med.
892		819 Baby Pink-lt.
24		776 Pink-med.
66		3688 Mauve-med.
69		3687 Mauve
95		554 Violet-lt.
98		553 Violet-med.
158		747 Sky Blue-vy. lt.

158		828 Blue Ultra-vy. lt.
159		827 Blue-vy. lt.
160		813 Blue-lt.
145		334 Baby Blue-med.
147		312 Navy Blue-lt.
203		564 Jade-vy. lt.
210		562 Jade-med.
397		453 Shell Gray-lt.
399		452 Shell Gray-med.

Step 2: Backstitch (one strand)

70		3685 Mauve-dk. (berries)
879		890 Pistachio Green-ultra dk. (leaves, stems)
401		844 Beaver Gray-ultra dk. (all else)

Step 3: French Knots (one strand)

401		844 Beaver Gray-ultra dk.

continued . . .

57

MATERIALS

Completed cross-stitch on white
  Linda 27; matching thread
⅜ yard of 45″-wide blue pin-dot
  fabric; matching thread
12″ x 12″ piece of muslin fabric
12″ x 12″ piece of polyester
  batting
1½ yards of 1½″-wide flat white
  cotton lace
⅞ yard of ½″-wide white lace
¾ yard of ⅝″-wide white lace
4 yards of ⅛″-wide white satin
  ribbon
1¾ yards of 1/16″-wide rose satin
  ribbon
12″ x 12″ knife-edge pillow form
1⅜ yards of small cording
Dressmakers' pen or chalk
Large-eyed needle

DIRECTIONS

1. Cut the Linda 8″ x 8″, with the design centered.

2. From the blue pin-dot fabric, cut two 12″ squares. Also cut a 1½″-wide bias strip, piecing as needed, to equal 48″. Cover the cording (see General Instructions).

3. Layer the muslin, batting, and one piece of the blue pin-dot fabric (right side up) for the pillow top. Baste together. With chalk or dressmakers' pen, mark diagonal quilting lines ½″ apart on blue pin-dot fabric. Quilt by hand.

4. Press under ½″ around the edges of the Linda. Baste the ½″-wide lace under the edge of the Linda, easing in fullness at corners. Center the Linda on the quilted top and slipstitch in place.

5. With a dressmakers' pen, mark 1″ inside and parallel to the folded edge of the Linda. Using this line as a guide, slipstitch the ⅝″-wide lace to the Linda, easing in fullness at corners.

6. With raw edges aligned, stitch the cording to the right side of the pillow top with a ½″ seam.

7. With right sides together, stitch the pillow front to the back, sewing on the stitching line of the cording. Leave a 10″ opening on one side. Trim the seams and turn right side out. Insert the pillow form and slipstitch the opening closed.

8. Place the 1½″-wide lace around the back of the pillow and slipstitch to the back of the cording.

9. Cut one 64″ length of ⅛″-wide white ribbon and thread it through the large-eyed needle. Run the ribbon through the lace around the pillow next to the cording. Leave 10″ of ribbon extending at the beginning and the end.

10. Cut one 24″ length of ⅛″-wide ribbon; set aside. With the remaining length of ribbon, make five loops, each 2½″ across. To form a bow, tie the 24″ length of ribbon around the center of the loops. Tack the bow to the edge of the pillow where the threaded ribbon extends. Tie these ends around the bow. Trim the ribbons to the desired length and tie a knot in each loose end.

11. Cut one 24″ length of 1/16″-wide ribbon. Thread it through the needle and run it through the ⅝″-wide lace, leaving a 2″ end extending at the beginning and the end. Cut one 12″ length of 1/16″ wide ribbon; set aside. With the remaining length of ribbon, form five 2″ figure eights. Tie the 12″ length around the center of the figure eights to make a bow. Tack the bow to the pillow and tie the loose ends of the threaded ribbon around it. Trim the ribbons to the desired length and tie a knot in each loose end.

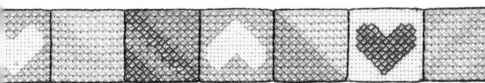

❖

MAY 1 - 7
National Pet Week

Whether your pet is a soft little chick or a lovable pony, it's a friend. You can help your friend by promoting an awareness of animal health and care during this week. And for your favorite young pet lover, stitch this sampler as a reminder of the week.

continued . . .

Stitch Count: 120 x 150

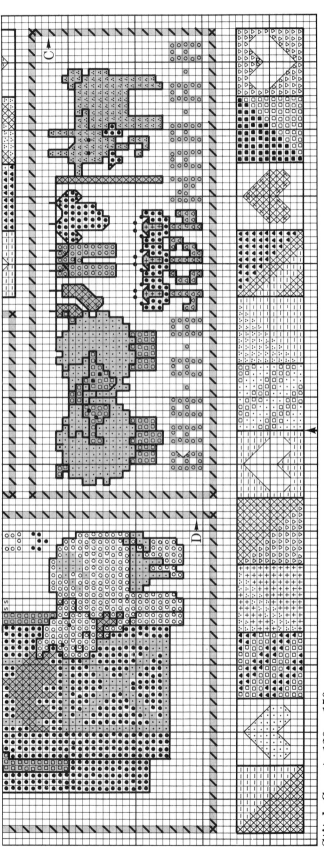

A Barnful of Pets

SAMPLE

Stitched on cream Hardanger 22 over two threads, the finished design size is 10⅞" x 13¾". The fabric was cut 17" x 20".

Bates   **DMC (used for sample)**

Step 1: Cross-stitch (three strands)

1	z	White
306	☒	725 Topaz

778	▨	754 Peach Flesh-lt.
868	H	758 Terra Cotta-lt.
324	+	922 Copper-lt.
70	●	3685 Mauve-dk.
120	N	794 Cornflower Blue-lt.
940	◑	792 Cornflower Blue-dk.
243	▲	988 Forest Green-med.
926	·	Ecru
942	⊡	738 Tan-vy. lt.
363	○	436 Tan
392	s	642 Beige Gray-dk.
382	E	3371 Black Brown
401	▢	535 Ash Gray-vy. lt.
401	▣	535 Ash Gray-vy. lt. (French knot over cross-stitch)

Step 2: Filet Cross-stitch (one strand)

306	⠃	725 Topaz
868	─	758 Terra Cotta-lt.
70	☒	3685 Mauve-dk.
120	⋰	794 Cornflower Blue-lt.
940	◼	792 Cornflower Blue-dk.
243	◀	988 Forest Green-med.
942	▢	738 Tan-vy. lt.
392	▷	642 Beige Gray-dk.
401	+	535 Ash Gray-vy. lt.

Step 3: Backstitch (one strand)

382	⌐	3371 Black Brown

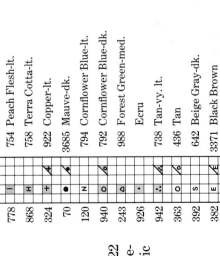

Step 4: French Knots (one strand)

382	●	3371 Black Brown
382	⊡	3371 Black Brown

Step 5: Ribbonwork (⅛"-wide ribbon couched with matching thread)

	╱	Blue (A)
	╱	Yellow (B)
	╱	Brown (C)
	╱	Green (D)

FABRICS   **DESIGN SIZES**
Aida 11   10⅞" x 13¾"
Aida 14   8⅝" x 10¾"
Aida 18   6⅝" x 8¼"
Hardanger 22   5½" x 6¾"

MAY 8
Mother's Day

A mother's love is unique in every family, and this day is set aside just for her. So shower her with attention and handmade gifts. The idea for this holiday was proposed by Anna Jarvis of Philadelphia in 1907. She requested that her church hold a service on the anniversary of her own mother's death, in memory of all mothers.

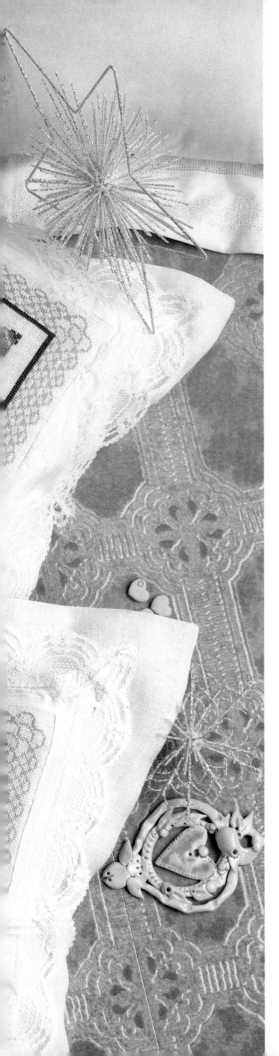

Heart & Star Pillows

SAMPLES
Stitched on white Belfast Linen 32 over two threads, the finished design size is 8⅛" x 7½". The fabric was cut 18" x 18". Use the outer border from the heart pillow pattern around the star (see photo).

FABRICS	DESIGN SIZES
Aida 11	11⅞" x 10⅞"
Aida 14	9¼" x 8⅝"
Aida 18	7¼" x 6⅝"
Hardanger 22	5⅞" x 5½"

MATERIALS (for one pillow)
Completed cross-stitch on white Belfast Linen 32; matching thread
One 15½" x 15½" piece of white Belfast Linen or other fabric for back
One 12" x 12" white handkerchief with lace trim
One 10" x 10" white handkerchief with lace trim
¾ yard of ⅜"-wide white lace for bow (on heart pillow)
One 12" x 12" knife-edge pillow form
Dressmakers' pen

DIRECTIONS
1. Cut the stitched linen 15½" x 15½", with the design centered. Make a line ¼" outside and around the design with a dressmakers' pen.

2. Center the 12" x 12" handkerchief over the stitched design. Pin the outside edge of the handkerchief to the linen. With the dressmakers' pen, trace the pen line marked on the linen onto the handkerchief. Carefully cut the handkerchief ¼" inside this line. Discard the center of the handkerchief. Clip each inside corner of the remaining portion of the handkerchief to the pen line at a 45-degree angle. Fold edges under ¼" and slipstitch to the linen.

3. For the Star pillow, center the 10" x 10" handkerchief diagonally over the design. Repeat Step 2, stitching the second handkerchief over the first.
   For the Heart pillow, center the second handkerchief the same as the first, not diagonally. (To align the inside edges of the lace on the two handkerchiefs, it may be necessary to hand-stitch a tuck at each corner of the handkerchief.)

4. Fold the handkerchiefs toward the center of the design, away from the edge of the linen. With right sides together, stitch the pillow back to the front with a ½" seam. Leave a 10" opening. Turn right side out and press the edge.

5. Stitch 1½" inside the edge, leaving a 10" opening parallel to the first opening. Insert the pillow form. Complete the inside stitching line by hand or machine. Slipstitch the outer opening.

6. For the Heart pillow, cut one 10" length of lace. Fold the remaining lace into 4" loops. Tie the 10" length around the center of the lace loops to form a bow. Tack the bow to the pillow top and trim the ends.

continued . . .

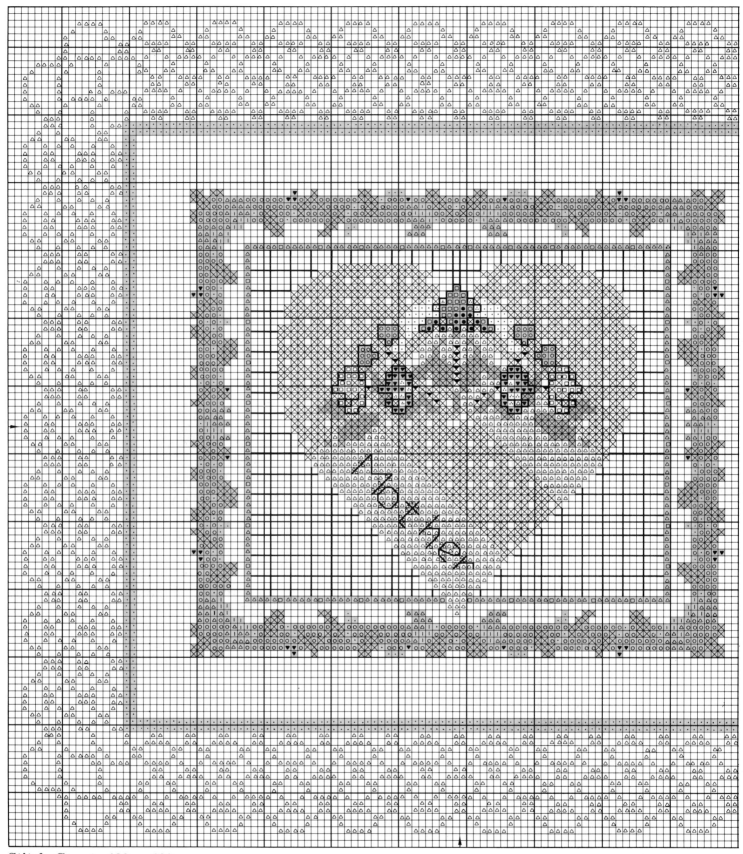

Stitch Count: 130 x 120

64

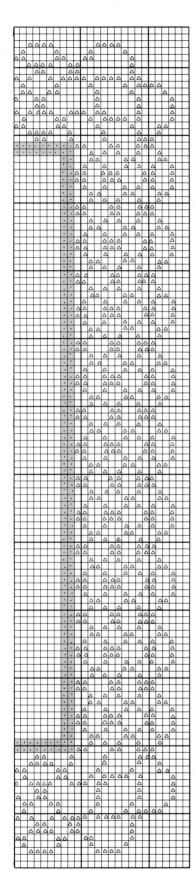

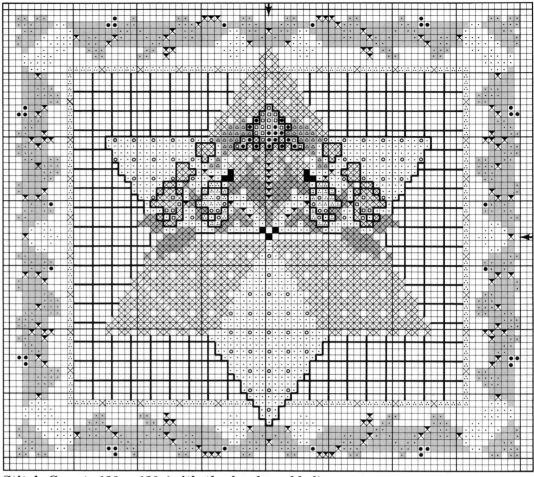

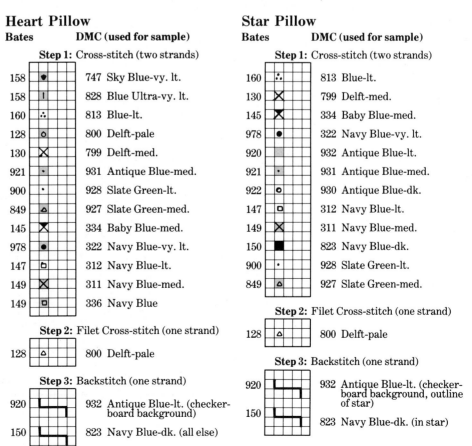

Stitch Count: 130 x 120 (with the border added)

Heart Pillow

Bates		DMC (used for sample)
		Step 1: Cross-stitch (two strands)
158	♥	747 Sky Blue-vy. lt.
158	I	828 Blue Ultra-vy. lt.
160	∴	813 Blue-lt.
128	o	800 Delft-pale
130	X	799 Delft-med.
921	•	931 Antique Blue-med.
900	·	928 Slate Green-lt.
849	△	927 Slate Green-med.
145	X	334 Baby Blue-med.
978	●	322 Navy Blue-vy. lt.
147	▫	312 Navy Blue-lt.
149	X	311 Navy Blue-med.
149	▫	336 Navy Blue
		Step 2: Filet Cross-stitch (one strand)
128	△	800 Delft-pale
		Step 3: Backstitch (one strand)
920		932 Antique Blue-lt. (checker-board background)
150		823 Navy Blue-dk. (all else)

Star Pillow

Bates		DMC (used for sample)
		Step 1: Cross-stitch (two strands)
160	∴	813 Blue-lt.
130	X	799 Delft-med.
145	X	334 Baby Blue-med.
978	●	322 Navy Blue-vy. lt.
920		932 Antique Blue-lt.
921	·	931 Antique Blue-med.
922	o	930 Antique Blue-dk.
147	▫	312 Navy Blue-lt.
149	X	311 Navy Blue-med.
150	■	823 Navy Blue-dk.
900	·	928 Slate Green-lt.
849	△	927 Slate Green-med.
		Step 2: Filet Cross-stitch (one strand)
128	△	800 Delft-pale
		Step 3: Backstitch (one strand)
920		932 Antique Blue-lt. (checker-board background, outline of star)
150		823 Navy Blue-dk. (in star)

Teacher Thank·You Week

Now is the perfect time to show your children's favorite teachers that you appreciate their hard work and dedication. Send one of these cross-stitched scenes along with a big, shiny red apple as a special thank-you.

The School Yard

SAMPLE
Stitched on white Aida 14, the finished design size is 9⅜″ x 11⅞″. The fabric was cut 16″ x 18″.

continued . . .

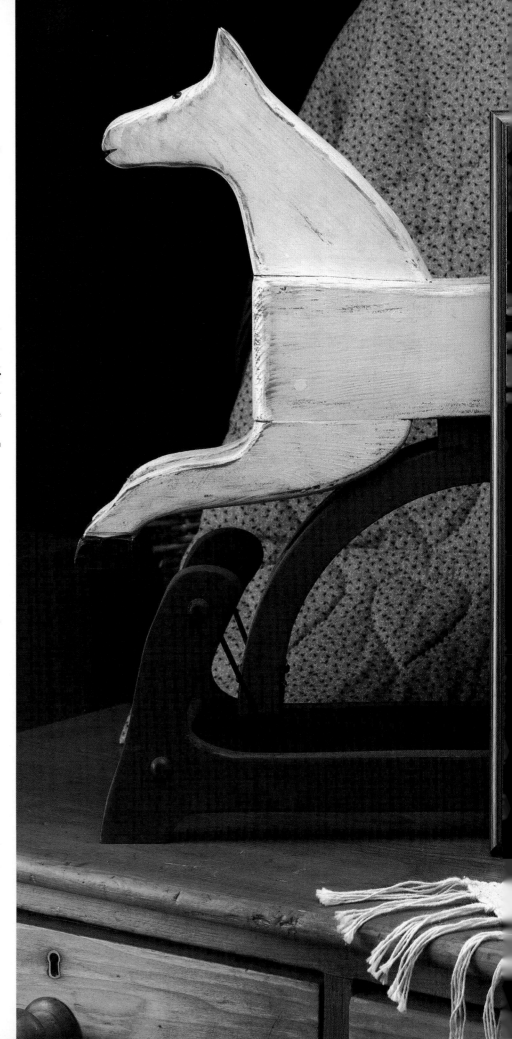

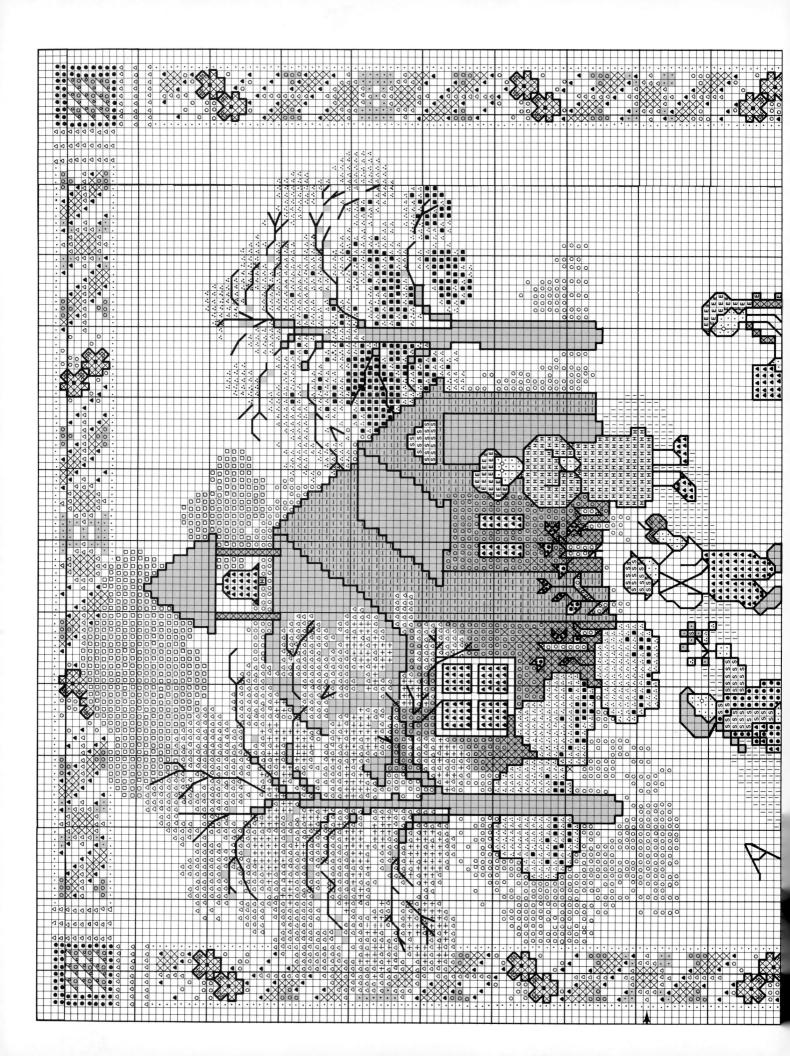

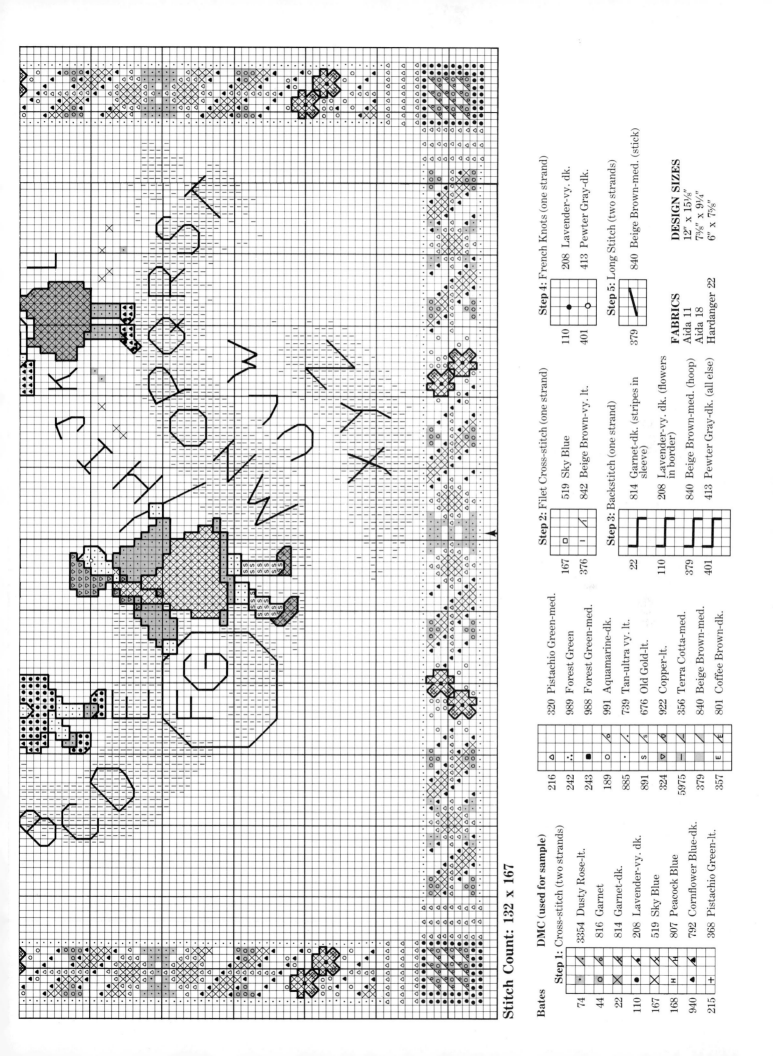

Stitch Count: 132 x 167

Step 4: French Knots (one strand)

110	Lavender-vy. dk.
401	Pewter Gray-dk.

Step 5: Long Stitch (two strands)

379	Beige Brown-med. (stick)

DESIGN SIZES
12" x 15⅛"
7⅜" x 9¼"
6" x 7⅝"

FABRICS
Aida 11
Aida 18
Hardanger 22

Step 2: Filet Cross-stitch (one strand)

167	Sky Blue
376	Beige Brown-vy. lt.

Step 3: Backstitch (one strand)

22	Garnet-dk. (stripes in sleeve)
110	Lavender-vy. dk. (flowers in border)
379	Beige Brown-med. (hoop)
401	Pewter Gray-dk. (all else)

216		Pistachio Green-med.
242		Forest Green
243		Forest Green-med.
189		Aquamarine-dk.
885		Tan-ultra vy. lt.
891	s	Old Gold-lt.
324		Copper-lt.
5975		Terra Cotta-med.
379		Beige Brown-med.
357		Coffee Brown-dk.

Bates **DMC (used for sample)**

Step 1: Cross-stitch (two strands)

74		3354	Dusty Rose-lt.
44		816	Garnet
22		814	Garnet-dk.
110		208	Lavender-vy. dk.
167		519	Sky Blue
168	H	807	Peacock Blue
940		792	Cornflower Blue-dk.
215	+	368	Pistachio Green-lt.

Stitch Count: 44 x 58

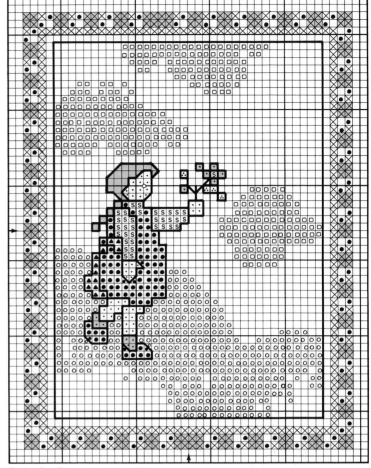

Stitch Count: 44 x 58

School Days

SAMPLES

Stitched on white Aida 14, the finished design size is 3⅛" x 4⅛". The fabric was cut 10" x 11".

Girl with a Book

Bates			DMC (used for sample)

Step 1: Cross-stitch (two strands)

Bates			DMC (used for sample)
74	·	/	3354 Dusty Rose-lt.
22	X	/	814 Garnet-dk.
110	●	/	208 Lavender-vy. dk.
940	▲	▲	792 Cornflower Blue-dk.
216	△	/	320 Pistachio Green-med.
189	○	/	991 Aquamarine-dk.
885	·	/	739 Tan-ultra vy. lt.
376	I	/	842 Beige Brown-vy. lt.
357	E	E	801 Coffee Brown-dk.

Step 2: Filet Cross-stitch (one strand)

167	□		519 Sky Blue

Step 3: Backstitch (one strand)

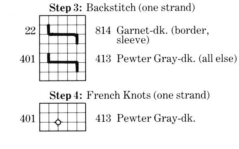

22		814 Garnet-dk. (border, sleeve)
401		413 Pewter Gray-dk. (all else)

Step 4: French Knots (one strand)

401	◇	413 Pewter Gray-dk.

Girl with Flowers

Bates			DMC (used for sample)

Step 1: Cross-stitch (two strands)

74	·	/	3354 Dusty Rose-lt.
22	X		814 Garnet-dk.
110	●	/	208 Lavender-vy. dk.
167	X		519 Sky Blue
940	▲		792 Cornflower Blue-dk.
242	∴		989 Forest Green
189	○	/	991 Aquamarine-dk.

885	·	/	739 Tan-ultra vy. lt.
891	s		676 Old Gold-lt.
379		/	840 Beige Brown-med.

Step 2: Filet Cross-stitch (one strand)

167	□		519 Sky Blue

Step 3: Backstitch (one strand)

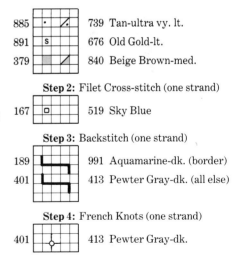

189		991 Aquamarine-dk. (border)
401		413 Pewter Gray-dk. (all else)

Step 4: French Knots (one strand)

401	◇	413 Pewter Gray-dk.

continued . . .

Stitch Count: 44 x 58

Stitch Count: 44 x 58

Girl with a Hoop

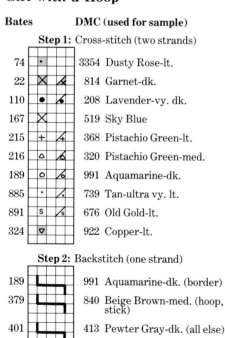

Bates			DMC (used for sample)
Step 1: Cross-stitch (two strands)			
74	·		3354 Dusty Rose-lt.
22	✕	◣	814 Garnet-dk.
110	●	◢	208 Lavender-vy. dk.
167	✕		519 Sky Blue
215	+	◢	368 Pistachio Green-lt.
216	△	◢	320 Pistachio Green-med.
189	○	◢	991 Aquamarine-dk.
885	·	◢	739 Tan-ultra vy. lt.
891	S	◢	676 Old Gold-lt.
324	▽		922 Copper-lt.

Step 2: Backstitch (one strand)

189		991 Aquamarine-dk. (border)
379		840 Beige Brown-med. (hoop, stick)
401		413 Pewter Gray-dk. (all else)

Step 3: French Knots (one strand)

401	○	413 Pewter Gray-dk.

Step 4: Long Stitch (one strand)

379	╱	840 Beige Brown-med. (stick)

Teacher and Boy

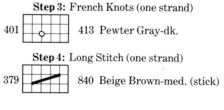

Bates			DMC (used for sample)
Step 1: Cross-stitch (two strands)			
22	✕	◢	814 Garnet-dk.
110	●	◢	208 Lavender-vy. dk.
167	✕		519 Sky Blue
168	H	◢	807 Peacock Blue
940	▲	◢	792 Cornflower Blue-dk.
242	∴	◢	989 Forest Green
189	○	◢	991 Aquamarine-dk.
885	·	◢	739 Tan-ultra vy. lt.
891	S	◢	676 Old Gold-lt.
379		╱	840 Beige Brown-med.
357	E	◢	801 Coffee Brown-dk.

Step 2: Backstitch (one strand)

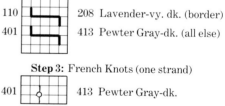

110		208 Lavender-vy. dk. (border)
401		413 Pewter Gray-dk. (all else)

Step 3: French Knots (one strand)

401	○	413 Pewter Gray-dk.

FABRICS	DESIGN SIZES
Aida 11	4" x 5¼"
Aida 18	2½" x 3¼"
Hardanger 22	2" x 2⅝"

JUNE 19

Father's Day

Remember Dad? He's the one
who shooed away the giants, who
taught you how to bait a hook,
and how to drive. On this day,
even grown-up children come
from far and near to honor him.

A Sampler
for Father

SAMPLE
Stitched on white Belfast Linen 32
over two threads, the finished design size is 9½" x 11½". The fabric
was cut 16" x 18".
continued . . .

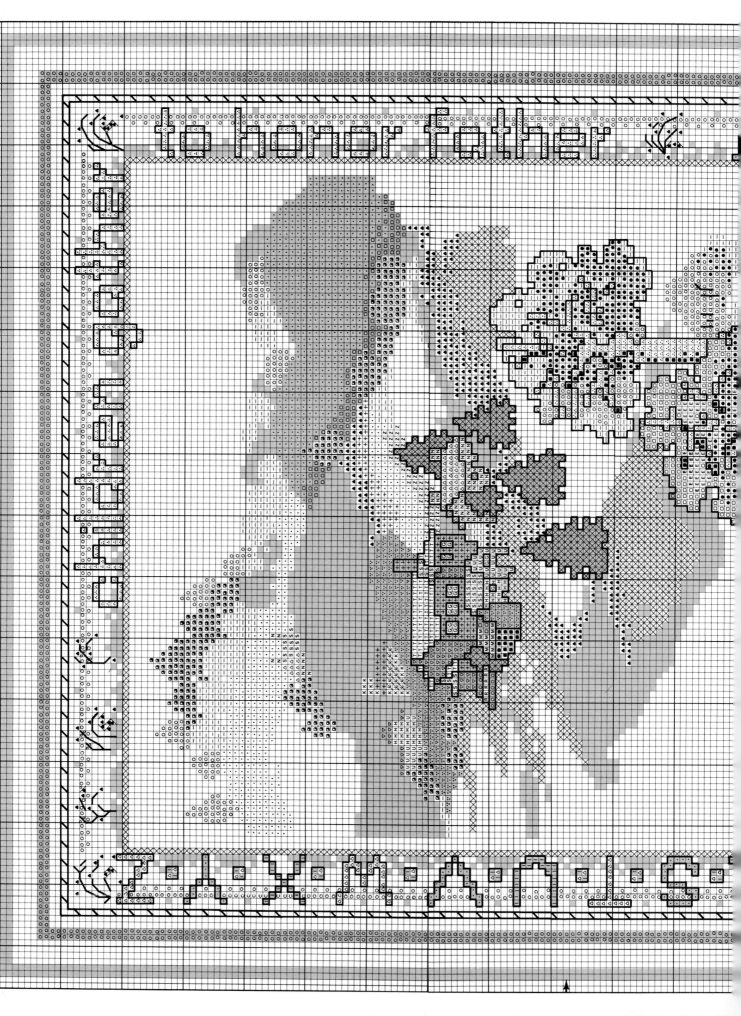

Stitch Count: 153 x 185

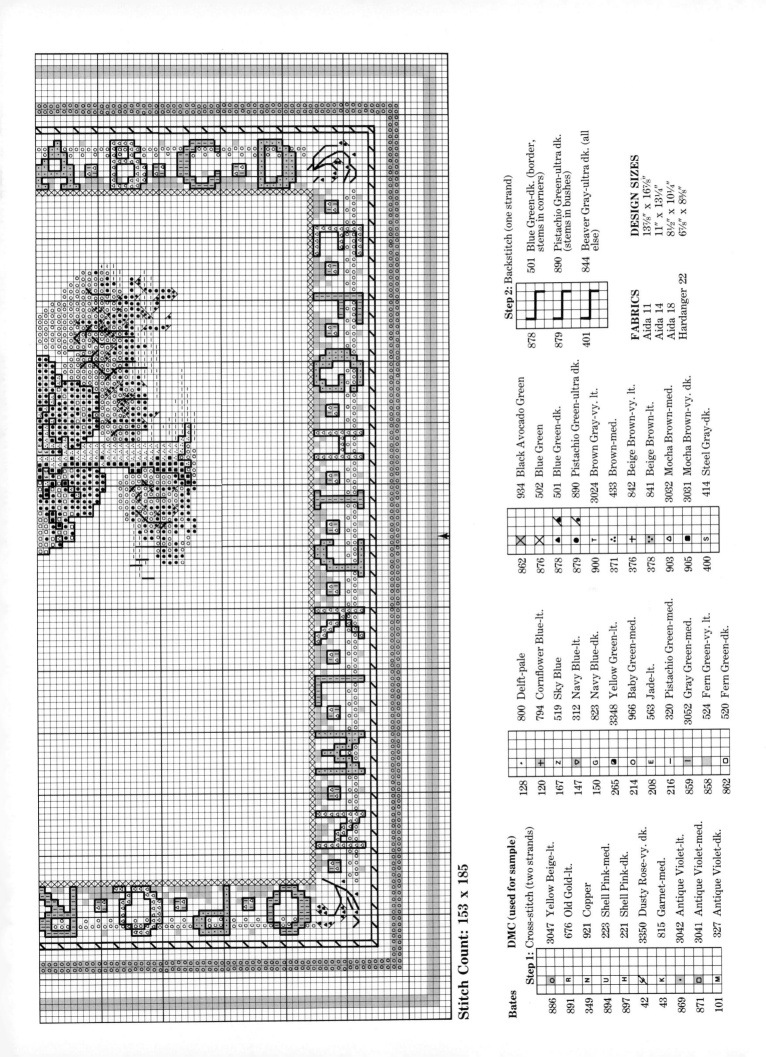

Bates		DMC (used for sample)
Step 1: Cross-stitch (two strands)		
886	·	3047 Yellow Beige-lt.
891	R	676 Old Gold-lt.
349	N	921 Copper
894	U	223 Shell Pink-med.
897	H	221 Shell Pink-dk.
42	✗	3350 Dusty Rose-vy. dk.
43	K	815 Garnet-med.
869	•	3042 Antique Violet-lt.
871	▢	3041 Antique Violet-med.
101	M	327 Antique Violet-dk.

128	·	800 Delft-pale
120	+	794 Cornflower Blue-lt.
167	z	519 Sky Blue
147	▷	312 Navy Blue-lt.
150	G	823 Navy Blue-dk.
265	◨	3348 Yellow Green-lt.
214	o	966 Baby Green-med.
208	E	563 Jade-lt.
216	—	320 Pistachio Green-med.
859			3052 Gray Green-med.
858		524 Fern Green-vy. lt.
862	□	520 Fern Green-dk.

862	⊠	934 Black Avocado Green
876	⊠	502 Blue Green
878	◀	501 Blue Green-dk.
879	●	890 Pistachio Green-ultra dk.
900	T	3024 Brown Gray-vy. lt.
371	∴	433 Brown-med.
376	+	842 Beige Brown-vy. lt.
378	∴	841 Beige Brown-lt.
903	◁	3032 Mocha Brown-med.
905	■	3031 Mocha Brown-vy. dk.
400	s	414 Steel Gray-dk.

Step 2: Backstitch (one strand)

878	501	Blue Green-dk. (border, stems in corners)
879	890	Pistachio Green-ultra dk. (stems in bushes)
401	844	Beaver Gray-ultra dk. (all else)

FABRICS   **DESIGN SIZES**

FABRICS	DESIGN SIZES
Aida 11	13⅞" x 16⅞"
Aida 14	11" x 13¼"
Aida 18	8½" x 10¼"
Hardanger 22	6⅞" x 8⅜"

JULY
State Fair Month

Baskets of summer-ripe fruits and vegetables are a sure sign that it's time to perfect that special recipe for the state fair. Tasty jams, jellies, pies, and breads will all vie for the coveted blue ribbons.

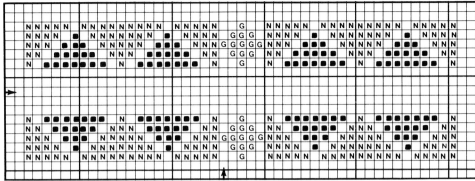

Stitch Count: 47 x 15

State Fair
Hand Towel

SAMPLE
Stitched on a natural brown/rose Town & Country towel, with the design centered at each end of the towel, the finished design size is 5″ x 1½″. As an option, the design may be stitched on cross-stitch fabric and topstitched on a purchased towel (see Materials and Directions).

Bates		DMC (used for sample)
		Step 1: Cross-stitch (three strands)
9	N	760 Salmon
128	G	800 Delft-pale
379	■	840 Beige Brown-med.

MATERIALS
Purchased linen or cotton hand or dish towel
Cross-stitch fabric to match towel

DIRECTIONS
1. Before cutting the cross-stitched fabric, measure the towel. Cut the cross-stitch fabric 2″ wider than the towel and 3″ higher than the height of the finished design.

2. Complete the stitching.

3. With the design centered, trim the band of cross-stitch fabric so that it is 1″ wider than the width of the towel and 1″ higher than the height of the design. Fold all edges under ¼″ and press.

4. Pin the band to the towel, placing the lower edge of the band 2½″ from the end of the towel. When using trim that has a raw edge (such as flat eyelet), place the edge under the band of cross-stitch. Topstitch the band to the towel, securing the edge of the trim.
    When using trim with finished edges, topstitch the band to the towel; then apply the trim.

At the Fair

SAMPLE
Stitched on cream Aida 14, the finished design size is 7″ x 9⅞″. The fabric was cut 13″ x 16″.

continued . . .

Stitch Count: 98 x 138

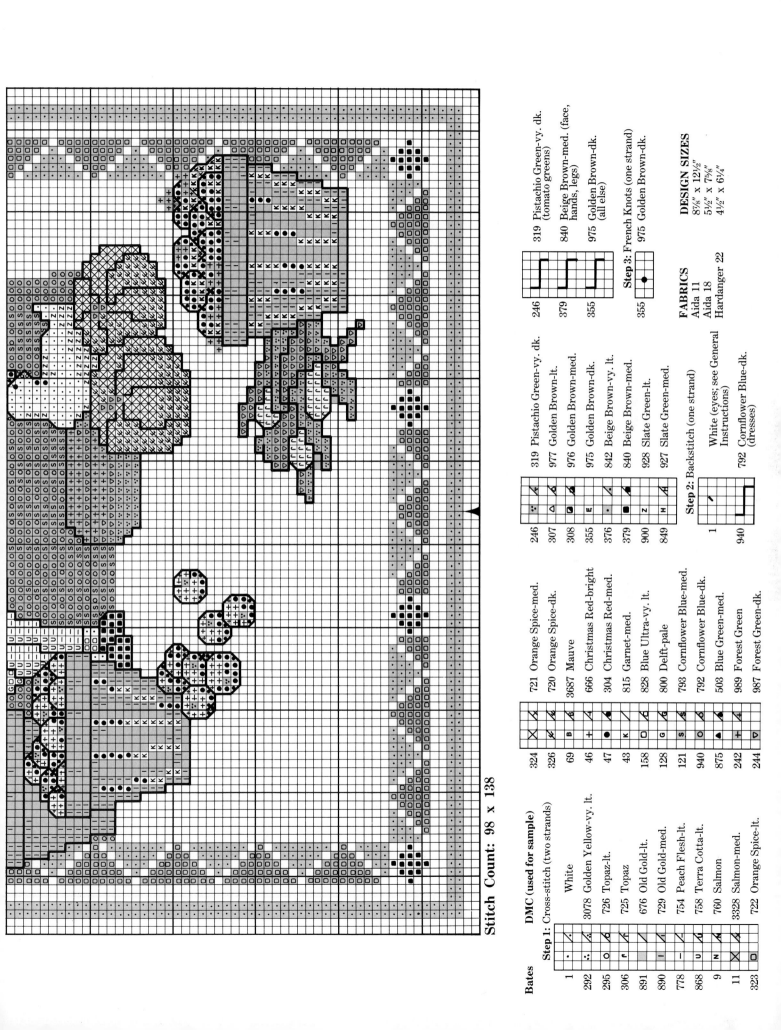

Bates	DMC (used for sample)
	Step 1: Cross-stitch (two strands)
1	White
292	3078 Golden Yellow-vy. lt.
295	726 Topaz-lt.
306	725 Topaz
891	676 Old Gold-lt.
890	729 Old Gold-med.
778	754 Peach Flesh-lt.
868	758 Terra Cotta-lt.
9	760 Salmon
11	3328 Salmon-med.
323	722 Orange Spice-lt.

Bates	DMC
324	721 Orange Spice-med.
326	720 Orange Spice-dk.
69	3687 Mauve
46	666 Christmas Red-bright
47	304 Christmas Red-med.
43	815 Garnet-med.
158	828 Blue Ultra-vy. lt.
128	800 Delft-pale
121	793 Cornflower Blue-med.
940	792 Cornflower Blue-dk.
875	503 Blue Green-med.
242	989 Forest Green
244	987 Forest Green-dk.

Bates	DMC
246	319 Pistachio Green-vy. dk.
307	977 Golden Brown-lt.
308	976 Golden Brown-med.
355	975 Golden Brown-dk.
376	842 Beige Brown-vy. lt.
379	840 Beige Brown-med.
900	928 Slate Green-lt.
849	927 Slate Green-med.

Step 2: Backstitch (one strand)

1	White (eyes; see General Instructions)
940	792 Cornflower Blue-dk. (dresses)

Bates	DMC
246	319 Pistachio Green-vy. dk. (tomato greens)
379	840 Beige Brown-med. (face, hands, legs)
355	975 Golden Brown-dk. (all else)

Step 3: French Knots (one strand)

355	975 Golden Brown-dk.

FABRICS
Aida 11
Aida 18
Hardanger 22

DESIGN SIZES
8⅞" x 12½"
5½" x 7⅞"
4½" x 6¼"

AUGUST 19
National Aviation Day

Orville Wright's birthday has been designated as National Aviation Day to commemorate the Wright brothers' contribution to aviation. Orville, with the help of his brother Wilbur, piloted the first self-powered flight in history on December 17, 1903. A more contemporary contribution to the field of aviation was that of three people from Albuquerque, New Mexico, who were the very first to complete a trans-Atlantic trip in a helium balloon. They finished their journey on August 17, 1978, after traveling some 3,200 miles in their craft, the Double Eagle II.

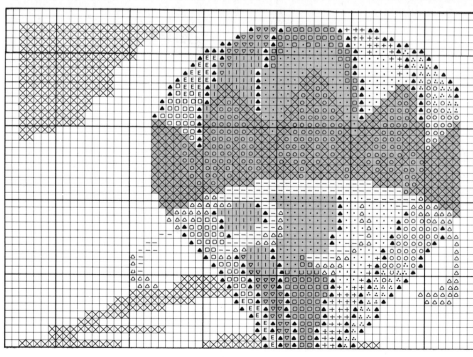

Up, Up, and Away!

SAMPLE
Stitched on white Aida 14, the finished design size is 4¼″ x 12⅛″. The fabric was cut 11″ x 19″.

Bates		DMC	(used for sample)
Step 1:		Cross-stitch (two strands)	
293	−	727	Topaz-vy. lt.
297	△	743	Yellow-med.
328	I	3341	Apricot
329	▽ ◿	3340	Apricot-med.
26	•	957	Geranium-pale
40	+	956	Geranium
76	▢	603	Cranberry
78	E	601	Cranberry-dk.
46	o ◿	666	Christmas Red-bright
47	✕ ◿	321	Christmas Red
95	o ◿	554	Violet-lt.
98	∴ ◿	553	Violet-med.
119	▲	333	Blue Violet-dk.
128	✕	800	Delft-pale
167	∵ ◿	598	Turquoise-lt.
206	·	955	Nile Green-lt.
208	▢	563	Jade-lt.
923	●	699	Christmas Green
875		503	Blue Green-med.
878	■	501	Blue Green-dk.
378	+	841	Beige Brown-lt.
379	s	840	Beige Brown-med.
380	H	839	Beige Brown-dk.
Step 2:		Backstitch (one strand)	
380	⌐	839	Beige Brown-dk.

FABRICS   **DESIGN SIZES**
Aida 11   5½″ x 15⅜″
Aida 18   3⅜″ x 9⅜″
Hardanger 22   2¾″ x 7¾″

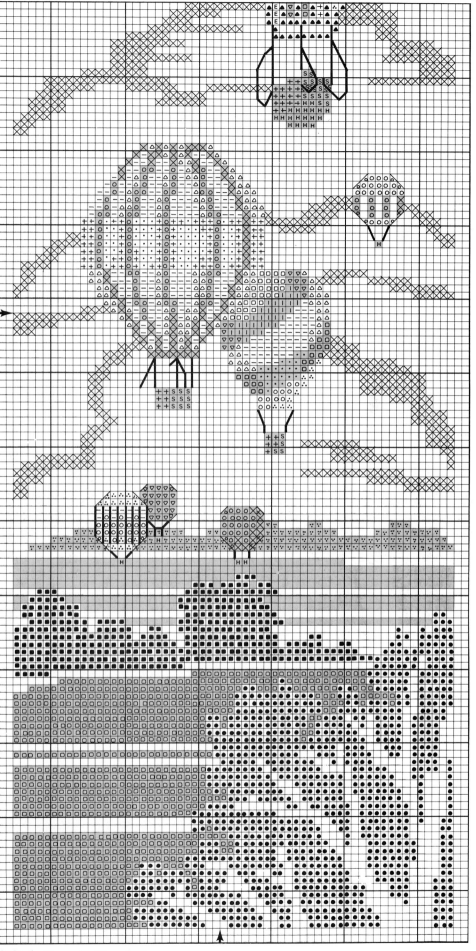

Stitch Count: 60 x 169

SEPTEMBER 11
Grandparents' Day

No one can brighten a day like grandparents! Their very presence can make us feel special and loved. Grandparents brag about our accomplishments and share in our joys. So remember them often, but especially on this September day.

Memories Photo Album

SAMPLE

Stitched on cream Belfast Linen 32 over two threads, the finished design size is 3¾" x 3⅛". The fabric was cut 7" x 9".

Stitch Count: 59 x 49

Bates		DMC (used for sample)
Step 1: Cross-stitch (two strands)		
48	·	818 Baby Pink
24	■	776 Pink-med.
215	X	368 Pistachio Green-lt.
885	o	739 Tan-ultra vy. lt.
Step 2: Backstitch (one strand)		
27		899 Rose-med. (flowers)
879		890 Pistachio Green-ultra dk. (lettering)
216		367 Pistachio Green-dk. (all else)
Step 3: French Knots (one strand)		
879	●	890 Pistachio Green-ultra dk.

FABRICS	DESIGN SIZES
Aida 11	5⅜" x 4½"
Aida 14	4¼" x 3½"
Aida 18	3¼" x 2¾"
Hardanger 22	2⅝" x 2¼"

MATERIALS

Completed cross-stitch on cream Belfast Linen 32
Photo album
½ yard of 45"-wide cream satin
½ yard of pink organza; matching thread
½ yard of polyester fleece
One large silk flower
1½ yards of ⅛"-wide green silk ribbon
Assorted memorabilia
Oval mat board, 5¾" x 4¾"
Two 12" x 12" pieces of cream medium-weight paper to line cover

Glue
Dressmakers' pen
Tracing paper for pattern

DIRECTIONS

1. Make the pattern for the oval. Trace the pattern onto the mat board and cut, or have the oval cut by a professional framer.

2. If possible, remove the photo pages from the album and set them aside. Place the tracing paper for the album cover pattern on a flat surface. Open the album and place it flat on the paper. Trace around the outside edge; then cut out the pattern.

3. From the fleece, cut one oval. Glue to the oval mat board. Also cut one piece of fleece ¼" larger on all edges than the pattern for the album cover. Glue to the album cover.

4. Center the oval pattern over the stitched design. Cut the linen 2" larger all around than the pattern. Sew a running stitch all around, ¼" from the edge of the linen. Place the fleece side of the oval against the wrong side of the design. Gather the linen around the mat, keeping the design centered. Secure the gathering thread and glue the edges of the linen to the mat. Set aside.

5. Cut one piece each of satin and organza, cutting each piece 2½" larger on all sides than the album pattern.

continued . . .

6. Open the album and center it against the wrong side of the satin piece. Run a line of glue along the inside of the ends of the album, ½″ from the edge and to within 1″ of album corners. Wrap satin around the ends, keeping fabric smooth but not tight. Test the tension by gently closing album.

At the top and bottom of the spine, clip the satin on each side of the center metal binder. Tuck the fabric under the binder (a paring knife or nail file may be helpful). Run a line of glue across the top and bottom edges of the album cover. Wrap the fabric around the top and bottom, checking the tension before glue sets. Leave corners loose until the glue is dry.

7. Repeat Step 6 with organza over the satin.

8. Pinch the fabric together at the corners, handling both layers as one, and glue in place.

9. Now cut the album pattern so it's the size of the front of the album. Trace this pattern onto both pieces of the cream paper. Cut ⅛″ inside tracing lines. Glue paper inside front and back covers, concealing all fabric edges.

10. Cut one 18″ length of silk ribbon. Fold the remaining ribbon into 3″ loops. Tie the 18″ length around the flower stem and around the center of the loops. Curl the ribbon ends by carefully running the ribbon over the sharp edge of one blade of a scissors.

11. Arrange the items on the front of the album, placing stitched oval, silk flower, and other large items first. Then fill in the spaces with smaller pieces. Glue the oval piece to the cover. Tack the flower stem in two places. Glue or tack remaining pieces as desired.

SEPTEMBER 17 —OCTOBER 2
Summer Olympics

It was in 776 B.C. that athletes from ancient Greece participated in the foot races of the first Olympic games. It wasn't long before other athletic events were added. The games were held every four years for 1,168 years and then were revived during the 1890s. This year, some 160 nations will be in Seoul, South Korea, to participate in this world event.

continued . . .

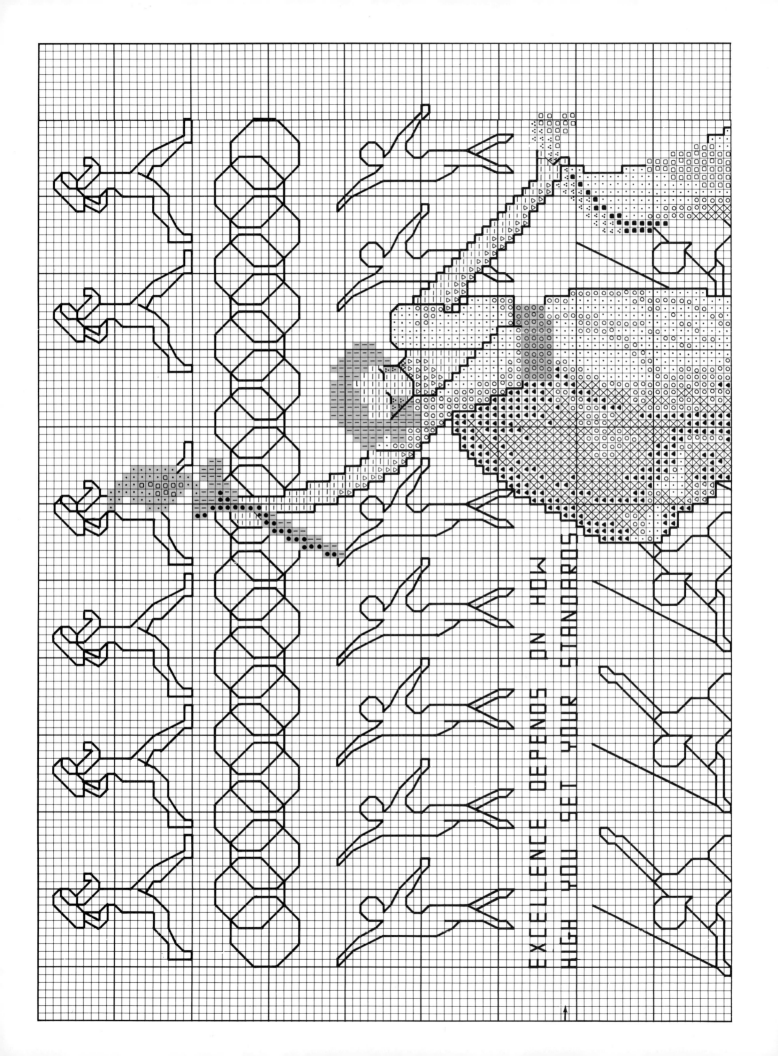

EXCELLENCE DEPENDS ON HOW HIGH YOU SET YOUR STANDARDS

Stitch Count: 123 x 133

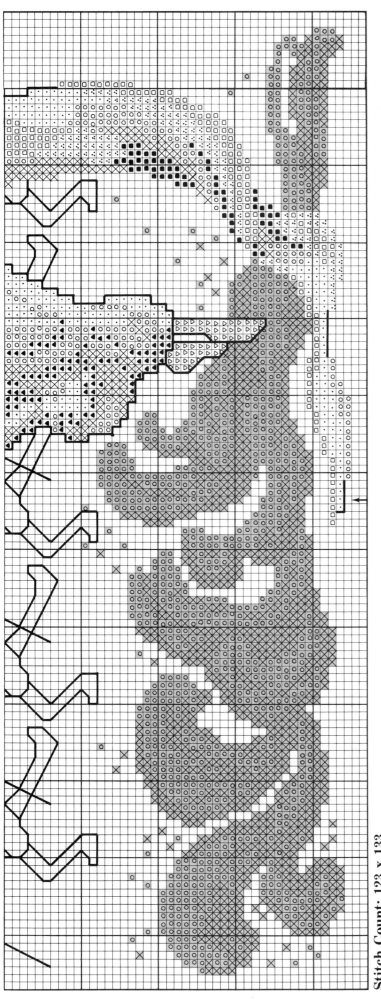

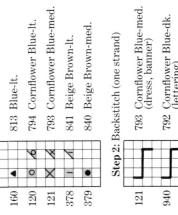

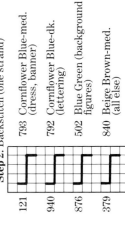

DESIGN SIZES

FABRICS	
Aida 11	11⅛" x 12⅛"
Aida 14	8¾" x 9½"
Aida 18	6⅞" x 7⅜"
Hardanger 22	5⅝" x 6"

Bates		DMC (used for sample)
	Step 1:	Cross-stitch (two strands)
1	·	White
298	·	972 Canary-deep
324	□	721 Orange Spice-med.
778	–	754 Peach Flesh-lt.
868	▷	758 Terra Cotta-lt.
8	∴	761 Salmon-lt.
42	□	335 Rose
59	∴	326 Rose-vy. deep
43	■	815 Garnet-med.
158	○	828 Blue Ultra-vy. lt.
159	✕	827 Blue-vy. lt.
160	◣	813 Blue-lt.
120	⊘	794 Cornflower Blue-lt.
121	⊠	793 Cornflower Blue-med.
378	⟋	841 Beige Brown-lt.
379	●	840 Beige Brown-med.

Step 2: Backstitch (one strand)

121		793 Cornflower Blue-med. (dress, banner)
940		792 Cornflower Blue-dk. (lettering)
876		502 Blue Green (background figures)
379		840 Beige Brown-med. (all else)

The Olympic Goddess

SAMPLE

Stitched on white Belfast Linen 32 over two threads, the finished design size is 7¾" x 8¼". The fabric was cut 14" x 15".

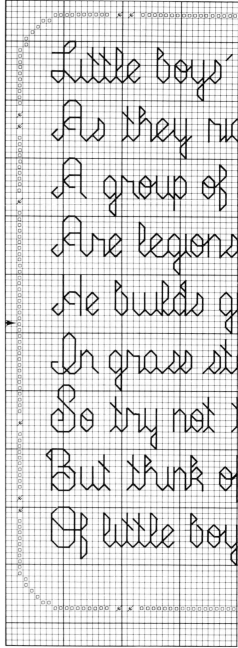

Stitch Count: 165 x 107

OCTOBER 3
Universal Children's Day

Little Boys' Dreams

Children in every land have their dreams. Universal Children's Day was set aside by the United Nations to honor children and to remind us of their needs and dreams.

SAMPLE
Stitched on white Linda 27 over two threads, the finished design size is 12¼" x 7⅞". The fabric was cut 19" x 14".

FABRICS	DESIGN SIZES
Aida 11	15" x 9¾"
Aida 14	11¾" x 7⅝"
Aida 18	9⅛" x 6"
Hardanger 22	7½" x 4⅞"

Bates		DMC (used for sample)
	Step 1: Cross-stitch (two strands)	
1	†	White
881	· /	945 Sportsman Flesh
301	△	744 Yellow-pale
297	∴ /	743 Yellow-med.
303	s	742 Tangerine-lt.
894	O	223 Shell Pink-med.

88

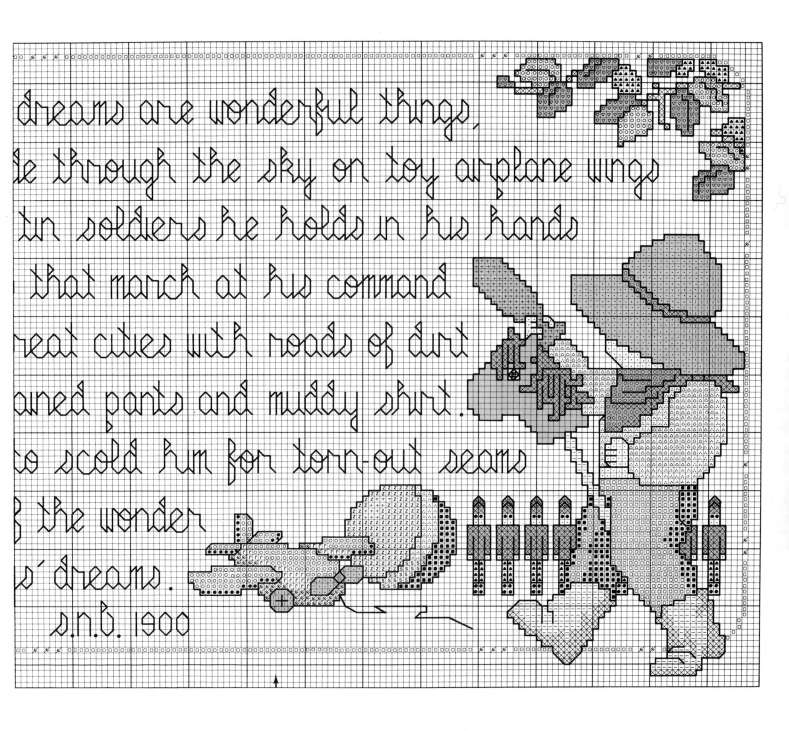

897		221 Shell Pink-dk.
159		3325 Baby Blue
145		334 Baby Blue-med.
978		322 Navy Blue-vy. lt.
242		989 Forest Green
244		987 Forest Green-dk.
246		986 Forest Green-vy. dk.
876		502 Blue Green

879		500 Blue Green-vy. dk.
362		437 Tan-lt.
309		435 Brown-vy. lt.
914		3064 Sportsman Flesh-med.
936		632 Negro Flesh
382		3371 Black Brown
8581		3022 Brown Gray-med.
398		415 Pearl Gray

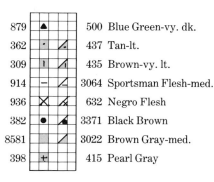

Step 2: Backstitch (one strand)

879		500 Blue Green-vy. dk. (lettering)
382		3371 Black Brown (all else)

Step 3: French Knots (one strand)

879		500 Blue Green-vy. dk. (lettering)

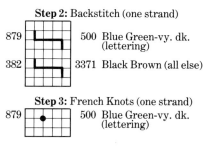

Little Girls' Dreams

SAMPLE

Stitched on white Linda 27 over two threads, the finished design size is 12¼" x 7⅞". The fabric was cut 19" x 14".

Bates			DMC (used for sample)

Step 1: Cross-stitch (two strands)

1	·	╱	White
880	–	╱	948 Peach Flesh-vy. lt.
881	∵	╱	945 Sportsman Flesh
301	·	╱	744 Yellow-pale
303	ı	╱	742 Tangerine-lt.
24	o	╱	776 Pink-med.
74	✕	╱	3354 Dusty Rose-lt.
894	●	╱	223 Shell Pink-med.
104	△		210 Lavender-med.
101	▼	╱	327 Antique Violet-dk.
159	▱		827 Blue-vy. lt.
876	▨	╱	502 Blue Green
914	⊙	╱	3064 Sportsman Flesh-med.
936	✕	╱	632 Negro Flesh
397	+	╱	762 Pearl Gray-vy. lt.

Step 2: Backstitch (one strand)

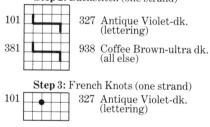

101	327 Antique Violet-dk. (lettering)
381	938 Coffee Brown-ultra dk. (all else)

Step 3: French Knots (one strand)

101	●	327 Antique Violet-dk. (lettering)

FABRICS — **DESIGN SIZES**

Aida 11	15" x 9⅝"
Aida 14	11¾" x 7⅝"
Aida 18	9⅛" x 5⅞"
Hardanger 22	7½" x 4⅞"

Stitch Count: 165 x 106

dreams are wonderful things,
ded grass circles are diamond rings.
t teas and fanciest balls
ed by teddy bears and dolls
allerina who flits on tip toe
y pink slippers and an old Christmas bow.
to scold her for girlish schemes
the wonder
s' dreams.

OCTOBER 15
Sweetest Day

Make somebody happy! That's what Herbert Kingston had in mind when he started this holiday over 60 years ago. Mr. Kingston, an employee of a candy company, distributed candy and other small gifts to the underprivileged in Cleveland to show them that somebody cared. Since then, other cities around the country have joined in, making this an occasion for remembering others with a kind deed.

Happy Play

SAMPLE

Stitched on white Belfast Linen 32 over two threads, the finished design size is 9½″ x 7¾″. The fabric was cut 16″ x 14″.

Happy Hearts Hand Towel

SAMPLE

Stitch on a rose Victoria towel (see Suppliers), using the graph for Happy Play. Center the design in the Aida areas of the towel and stitch the words "Happy Hearts." On both sides of the words (see photo), stitch the flower motif that appears immediately to the left of "Happy Hearts" in the graph. As an option, the design may be stitched on cross-stitch fabric and applied to a purchased towel (see State Fair Hand Towel, page 77).

continued . . .

Bates			DMC (used for sample)

Step 1: Cross-stitch (two strands)

Bates			DMC
885	−		739 Tan-ultra vy. lt.
373	+		422 Hazel Nut Brown-lt.
892	·		225 Shell Pink-vy. lt.
74	O		3354 Dusty Rose-lt.
27	∴		899 Rose-med.
894	+		223 Shell Pink-med.
69	▲		3687 Mauve
970			315 Antique Mauve-dk.
22	O		814 Garnet-dk.
869	H		3042 Antique Violet-lt.
105	△		209 Lavender-dk.
99			552 Violet-dk.
159			3325 Baby Blue
145	X		334 Baby Blue-med.
921	E		931 Antique Blue-med.
922	S		930 Antique Blue-dk.
940	■		792 Cornflower Blue-dk.
168	N		807 Peacock Blue
213	·		369 Pistachio Green-vy. lt.
215	▽		368 Pistachio Green-lt.
875	⌐		503 Blue Green-med.
876	X		502 Blue Green
878	●		501 Blue Green-dk.
392	◻		642 Beige Gray-dk.
903	K		640 Beige Gray-vy. dk.
378	U		841 Beige Brown-lt.
380	Z		839 Beige Brown-dk.
905	B		3031 Mocha Brown-vy. dk.
900			648 Beaver Gray-lt.
8581	◻		647 Beaver Gray-med.
905	R		645 Beaver Gray-vy. dk.
400	S		414 Steel Gray-dk.

Step 2: Backstitch (one strand)

Bates			DMC
379			840 Beige Brown-med. (short tree)
380			838 Beige Brown-vy. dk. (tall tree)
400			414 Steel Gray-dk.(lettering)
905			645 Beaver Gray-vy. dk. (all else)

Step 3: French Knots (one strand)

Bates			DMC
905	●		645 Beaver Gray-vy. dk.

FABRICS   **DESIGN SIZES**
Aida 11   13¾″ x 11⅛″
Aida 14   11″ x 8¾″
Aida 18   8½″ x 6⅞″
Hardanger 22   6¾″ x 5⅝″

Stitch Count: 152 x 123

OCTOBER 29
Pumpkin Day

Remember crisp fall days and fields of pumpkins ripening on the vines? Hayrides, hauntings, and pumpkin carvings will all come to mind as you stitch your very own pumpkin patch. This sampler makes a great companion piece to The Apple Orchard, pictured on page 34.

The Pumpkin Harvest

SAMPLE
Stitched on yellow Canvas 22 over two threads, the finished design size is 12¾″ x 10¼″. The fabric was cut 19″ x 17″.

continued . . .

Bates		DMC (used for sample)

Step 1: Cross-stitch (three strands)

Bates	symbol	DMC	name
288	∴	445	Lemon-lt.
297	· /	743	Yellow-med.
303	△	742	Tangerine-lt.
316	●	740	Tangerine
891	✕	676	Old Gold-lt.
35	□	891	Carnation-dk.
47	Z	321	Christmas Red
875	▽	503	Blue Green-med.
258	⊠	904	Parrot Green-vy. dk.
246	∴	986	Forest Green-vy. dk.
879	■	890	Pistachio Green-ultra dk.
376	·	842	Beige Brown-vy. lt.
378	⊡	841	Beige Brown-lt.
363	–	436	Tan
309	○	435	Brown-vy. lt.
371		433	Brown-med.
324	+	922	Copper-lt.
349	⊙	921	Copper
339	+	920	Copper-med.
307	I	977	Golden Brown-lt.
308	S	976	Golden Brown-med.
357	H	801	Coffee Brown-dk.
400	▲ ◢	317	Pewter Gray

Step 2: Backstitch (two strands)

879		890	Pistachio Green-ultra dk. (one strand; pumpkin tendrils)
363		436	Tan (small trees, large tree)
309		435	Brown-vy. lt. (largest tree)

Step 3: Long Stitch (two strands)

357		801	Coffee Brown-dk. (hay bales)

Step 4: Beadwork

	N	Yellow
	E	Tangerine
	U	Jade Green

FABRICS

FABRICS	DESIGN SIZES
Aida 11	12¾″ x 10¼″
Aida 14	10″ x 8⅛″
Aida 18	7¾″ x 6¼″
Hardanger 22	6¼″ x 5⅛″

98

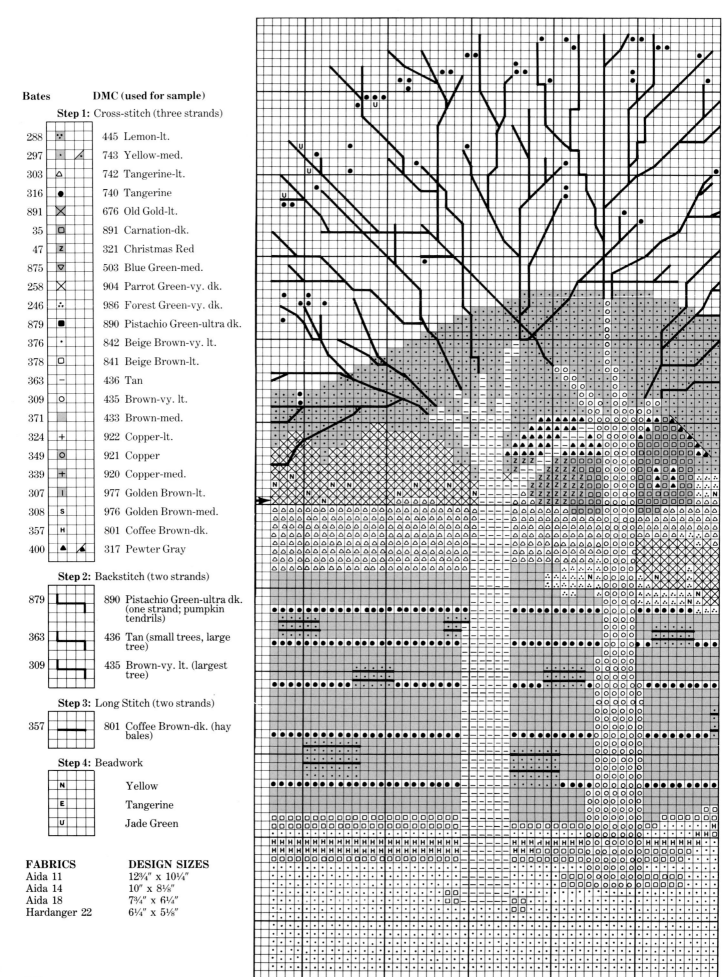

Stitch Count: 140 x 113

OCTOBER 31
Halloween

Lock the windows, bar the doors! The ghosts and goblins are out once more! But take a closer look and you'll probably see they're only the kids from down the street. They're ready for tricks and lots of treats with costumes and totes that can't be beat.

Halloween Totes

SAMPLES
The designs are stitched on ready-made tote bags, using Waste Canvas 14. Cut the waste canvas 3½″ x 3½″. Refer to Suppliers for information on ordering bags or see Materials and Directions to make your own bags.

continued . . .

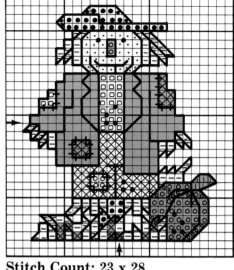

Stitch Count: 21 x 29

Stitch Count: 23 x 28

The Wizard: The finished design size is 1½" x 2⅛".

The Scarecrow: The finished design size is 1⅝" x 2".

Bates			DMC	(used for sample)
			Step 1: Cross-stitch (two strands)	
297	△		743	Yellow-med.
304	✕	◪	741	Tangerine-med.
98	✕	◪	553	Violet-med.
88	−	◪	718	Plum
131	·	◪	798	Delft-dk.
244	○	◪	987	Forest Green-dk.
942	I	◪	738	Tan-vy. lt.
363	▨	◪	436	Tan
403	●		310	Black

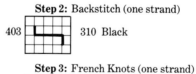

Step 2: Backstitch (one strand)

403		310 Black

Step 3: French Knots (one strand)

403	●	310 Black

FABRICS   **DESIGN SIZES**
Aida 11   1⅞" x 2⅝"
Aida 14   1½" x 2⅛"
Aida 18   1⅛" x 1⅝"
Hardanger 22   1" x 1⅜"

Bates			DMC	(used for sample)
			Step 1: Cross-stitch (two strands)	
301	·	◪	744	Yellow-pale
297	−	◪	743	Yellow-med.
304	○	◪	741	Tangerine-med.
330	□		947	Burnt Orange
19	○		817	Coral Red-vy. dk.
130	▨		809	Delft
255	I	◪	907	Parrot Green-lt.
244	✕	◪	987	Forest Green-dk.
363	✕	◪	436	Tan
351	●	◪	400	Mahogany-dk.

Step 2: Backstitch (one strand)

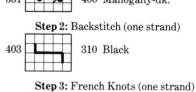

403		310 Black

Step 3: French Knots (one strand)

403	●	310 Black

FABRICS   **DESIGN SIZES**
Aida 11   2⅛" x 2½"
Aida 14   1⅝" x 2"
Aida 18   1¼" x 1½"
Hardanger 22   1" x 1¼"

Stitch Count: 30 x 30

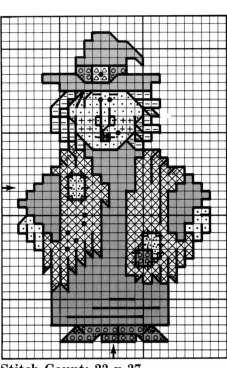

Stitch Count: 20 x 30

Stitch Count: 23 x 37

The Ghost: The finished design size is 2⅛" x 2⅛".

The Little Witch: The finished design size is 1⅜" x 2⅛".

The Big Witch: The finished design size is 1⅝" x 2⅝".

Bates		DMC (used for sample)	
Step 1: Cross-stitch (two strands)			
1		White	
304		741	Tangerine-med.
131		798	Delft-dk.
255		907	Parrot Green-lt.
397		762	Pearl Gray-vy. lt.
403		310	Black
Step 2: Backstitch (one strand)			
403		310	Black
Step 3: French Knots (one strand)			
403		310	Black

FABRICS **DESIGN SIZES**
Aida 11   2¾" x 2¾"
Aida 14   2⅛" x 2⅛"
Aida 18   1⅝" x 1⅝"
Hardanger 22 1⅜" x 1⅜"

Bates		DMC (used for sample)	
Step 1: Cross-stitch (two strands)			
778		754	Peach Flesh-lt.
297		743	Yellow-med.
316		740	Tangerine
8		761	Salmon-lt.
255		907	Parrot Green-lt.
399		318	Steel Gray-lt.
403		310	Black
Step 2: Backstitch (one strand)			
403		310	Black
Step 3: French Knots (one strand)			
403		310	Black

FABRICS **DESIGN SIZES**
Aida 11   1¾" x 2¾"
Aida 14   1⅜" x 2⅛"
Aida 18   1⅛" x 1⅝"
Hardanger 22 ⅞" x 1⅜"

Bates		DMC (used for sample)	
Step 1: Cross-stitch (two strands)			
301		744	Yellow-pale
9		760	Salmon
47		321	Christmas Red
159		827	Blue-vy. lt.
264		472	Avocado Green-ultra lt.
244		987	Forest Green-dk.
400		414	Steel Gray-dk.
403		310	Black
Step 2: Backstitch (one strand)			
403		310	Black
Step 3: French Knots (one strand)			
403		310	Black

FABRICS **DESIGN SIZES**
Aida 11   2⅛" x 3⅜"
Aida 14   1⅝" x 2⅝"
Aida 18   1¼" x 2"
Hardanger 22 1" x 1⅝"

continued . . .

MATERIALS (for one tote)
One 6″ x 13″ piece of cream
  canvas; matching thread
½ yard of 1″-wide cream
  webbing

DIRECTIONS
All seam allowances are ¼″.

1. Along one 13″ edge of the canvas, press ¼″ to the wrong side.

2. Cut the webbing into two equal lengths. Pin the raw ends to the wrong side of the canvas on the folded edge (Diagram A). Stitch ⅛″ from the fold, catching the ends of the webbing.

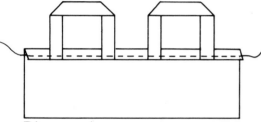

Diagram A

3. Fold the canvas with right sides together so that it measures 5¾″ x 6½″. Stitch down the side and across the bottom edge, backstitching at the beginning and end.

4. With the tote still inside out, align the side and bottom seams, forming a corner. Stitch across the corner (Diagram B). Form another corner on the opposite side of the tote and stitch. Turn the bag right side out, and it's ready for crossstitching.

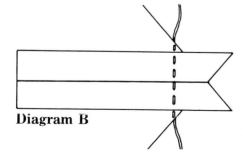

Diagram B

104

NOVEMBER 8
Election Day

Vote!

The first Tuesday after the first Monday in November is Presidential Election Day. So join the patriotic cause and display this sampler as a timely reminder!

SAMPLE
Stitched on white Aida 14, the finished design size is 8⅝" x 6¾". The fabric was cut 15" x 13".

continued . . .

Bates   **DMC (used for sample)**

Step 1: Cross-stitch (two strands)

1	·	⁄	White
42	∴		335 Rose
42	+		3350 Dusty Rose-vy. dk.
47	△	⁄	304 Christmas Red-med.
44	●	◢	816 Garnet
158	ı	⁄	775 Baby Blue-lt.
145	✕		334 Baby Blue-med.
978	○	◢	322 Navy Blue-vy. lt.
149	▲	◢	311 Navy Blue-med.
398	▨	⁄	415 Pearl Gray

Step 2: Filet Cross-stitch (one strand)

48	▦	818 Baby Pink

Step 3: Backstitch (one strand)

150	⌐	823 Navy Blue-dk.

FABRICS

Aida 11

Aida 18

Hardanger 22

DESIGN SIZES

10⅞" x 8⅝"

6⅝" x 5¼"

5½" x 4⅜"

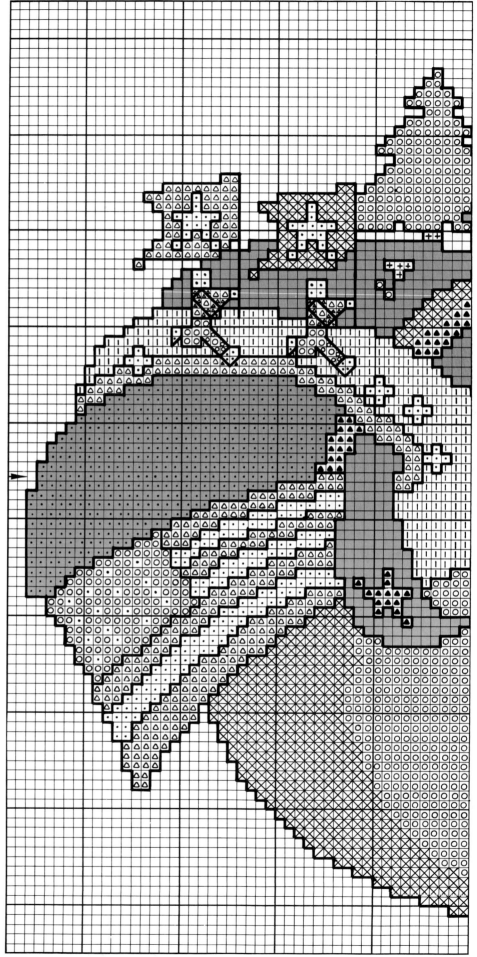

Stitch Count: 120 x 95

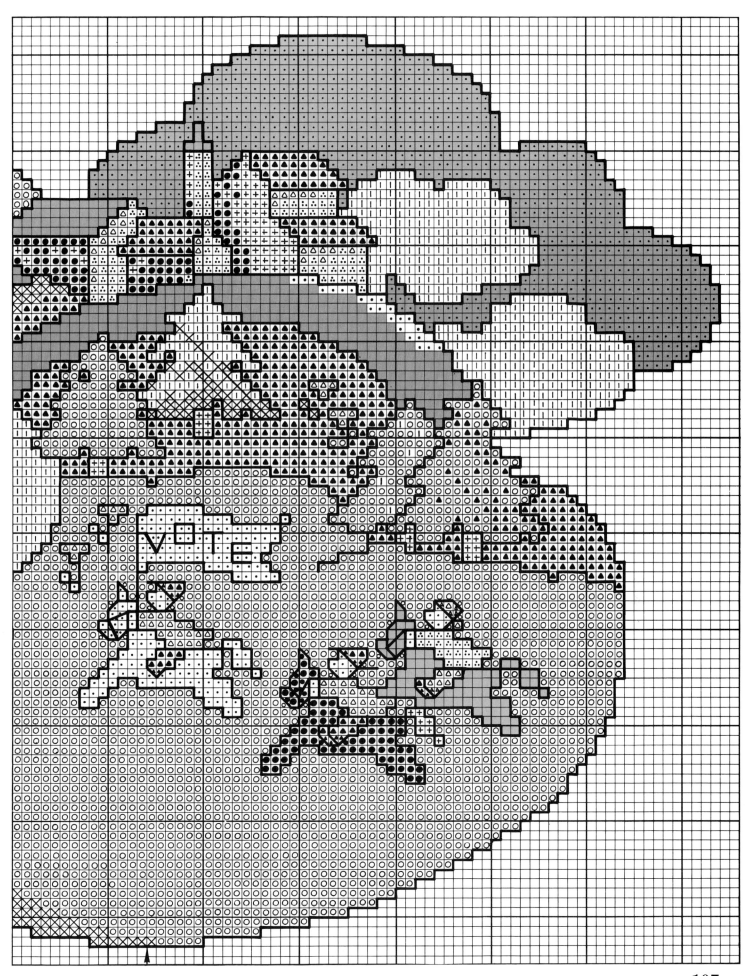

NOVEMBER 24
Thanksgiving

George Washington proclaimed November 26, 1786, as the first national Thanksgiving Day. Through the years, the holiday continued to be observed, but at different times in different areas. The custom of celebrating on the last Thursday of November was revived by President Lincoln. Today, however, we acknowledge the *fourth* Thursday of November (which is not always the last) as Thanksgiving Day, because of a resolution passed by Congress in 1941. This year, count your stitches and then count your blessings as you welcome family and friends gathering for the traditional feast.

Welcome Sampler

SAMPLE
Stitched on cream Belfast Linen 32 over two threads, the finished design size is 6″ x 8½″. The fabric was cut 12″ x 15″.

continued . . .

110

Stitch Count: 97 x 135

Bates **DMC (used for sample)**

continued . . . .

Step 1: Cross-stitch (two strands)

	Bates	DMC	
□	968	778	Antique Mauve-lt.
∷	894	223	Shell Pink-med.
▲	897	221	Shell Pink-dk.
◨	869	3042	Antique Violet-lt.
∷	871	3041	Antique Violet-med.
–	158	775	Baby Blue-lt.
·	120	794	Cornflower Blue-lt.
▷	168	518	Wedgewood-lt.
○	215	368	Pistachio Green-lt.

	Bates	DMC	
○	843	3364	Pine Green
⊠	876	502	Blue Green
●	878	501	Blue Green-dk.
⊠	212	561	Jade-vy. dk.
·	885	739	Tan-ultra vy. lt.
+	392	642	Beige Gray-dk.
▨	832	612	Drab Brown-med.
–	898	611	Drab Brown-dk.
◺	8581	646	Beaver Gray-dk.
■	401	535	Ash Gray-vy. lt.

Step 2: Backstitch (one strand)

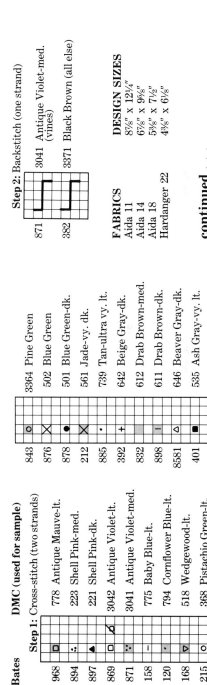

	871	3041	Antique Violet-med. (vines)
	382	3371	Black Brown (all else)

FABRICS   **DESIGN SIZES**
Aida 11   8⅞" x 12¼"
Aida 14   6⅞" x 9⅝"
Aida 18   5⅜" x 7½"
Hardanger 22   4⅜" x 6⅛"

Welcome Hand Towels

SAMPLES

For Empress Towels: Stitched on parchment Empress terry towels (available at needlework stores), the word "Welcome" and the house motif are centered in the provided space on one end. Stitch the house and trees as they appear on the graph, omitting the path and the blue background (see photo).

As an option, the designs may be stitched on cross-stitch fabric and topstitched on purchased cream terry cloth hand towels. Stitch the design on cream Aida 14. Calculate the finished design sizes (see General Instructions). Cut the Aida for each towel 3″ larger than the height of the design and 3″ wider than the width of the towel. Complete the stitching. (See the instructions for finishing the towels, page 77.)

112

DECEMBER 4
Hanukkah

This 2,000-year-old Jewish holiday is a time when families gather around a special Hanukkah menorah. For eight consecutive nights, a candle is lit in celebration of the Festival of Lights. It's a time when family members join together for songs, games, stories, presents, and prayers.

Happy Hanukkah

SAMPLE
Stitched on white Linda 27 over two threads, the finished design size is 10⅝" x 12⅛". The fabric was cut 17" x 18".

continued . . .

Stitch Count: 143 x 163

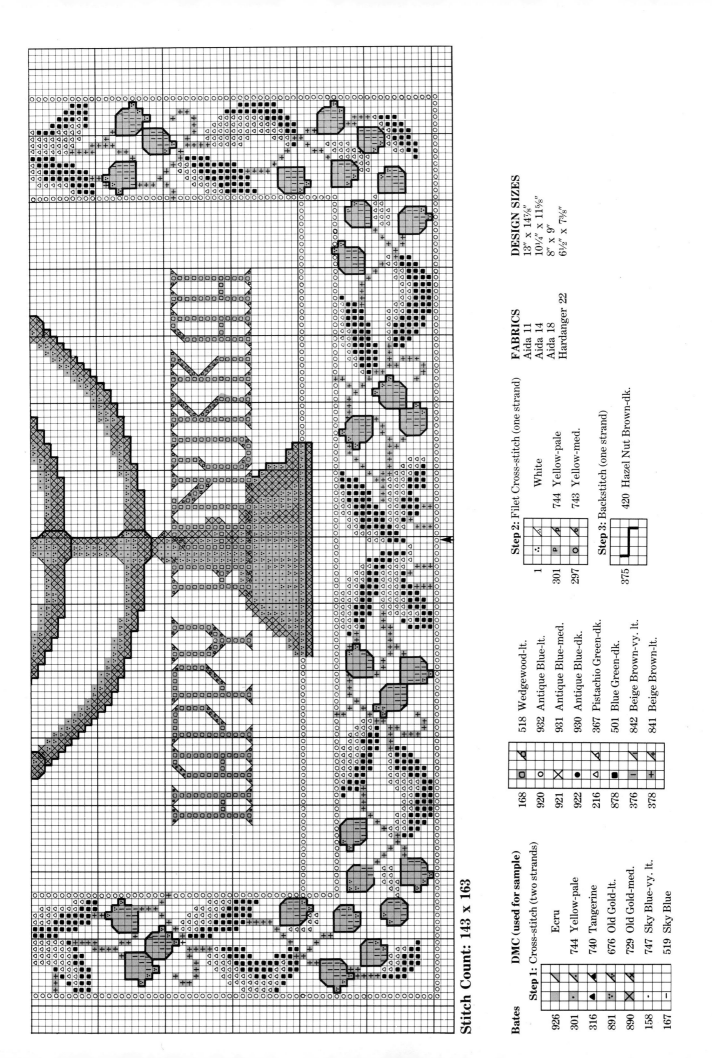

Bates   **DMC (used for sample)**

Step 1: Cross-stitch (two strands)

926			Ecru
744			Yellow-pale
740			Tangerine
316			Old Gold-lt.
891			Old Gold-med.
890			Sky Blue-vy. lt.
158			Sky Blue
167			Sky Blue

168		518 Wedgewood-lt.
920		932 Antique Blue-lt.
921		931 Antique Blue-med.
922		930 Antique Blue-dk.
216		367 Pistachio Green-dk.
878		501 Blue Green-dk.
376		842 Beige Brown-vy. lt.
378		841 Beige Brown-lt.

Step 2: Filet Cross-stitch (one strand)

1			White
301			744 Yellow-pale
297			743 Yellow-med.

Step 3: Backstitch (one strand)

375	420 Hazel Nut Brown-dk.

FABRICS
Aida 11
Aida 14
Aida 18
Hardanger 22

DESIGN SIZES
13" x 14⅞"
10¼" x 11⅝"
8" x 9"
6½" x 7⅜"

Christmas

Christmas is one of the most joyous days of the year. It is also one of the busiest seasons, with much of our time spent planning and preparing for special people. If you're looking for that perfect gift, why not cross-stitch a stocking, a sweatshirt, a quilt, or one of the other holiday designs? And remember, 'tis the season to be jolly, so deck the walls with cross-stitch and holly!

Christmas Goose Samplers

SAMPLES

Stitched on driftwood Belfast Linen 32 over two threads, the finished design size for each sampler is 6¼" x 10". For each design, the fabric was cut 13" x 16".

continued . . .

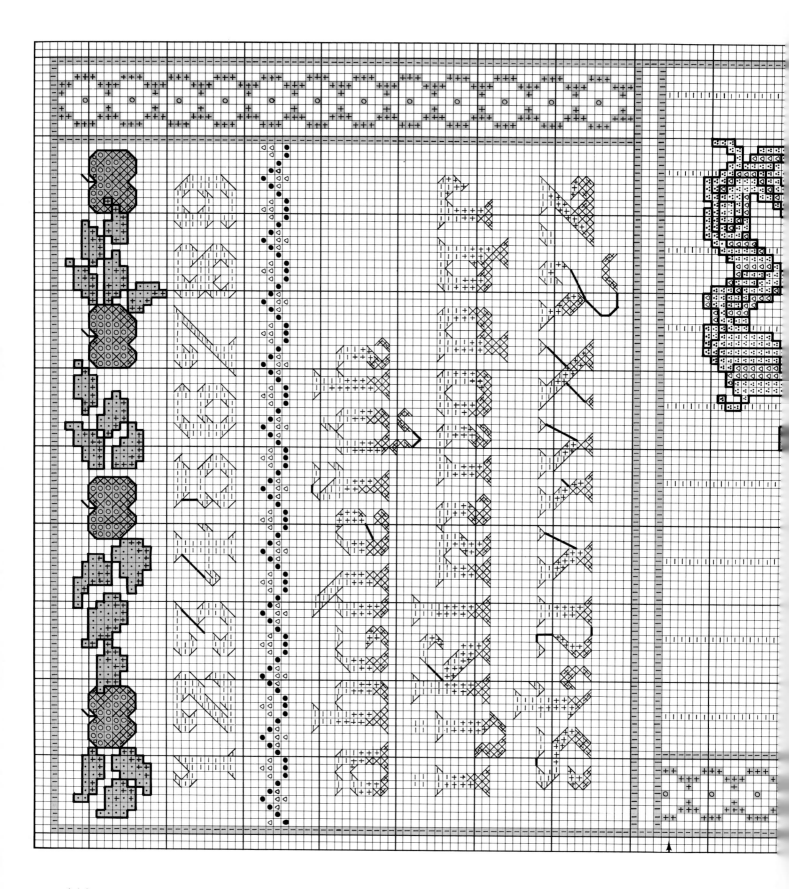

118

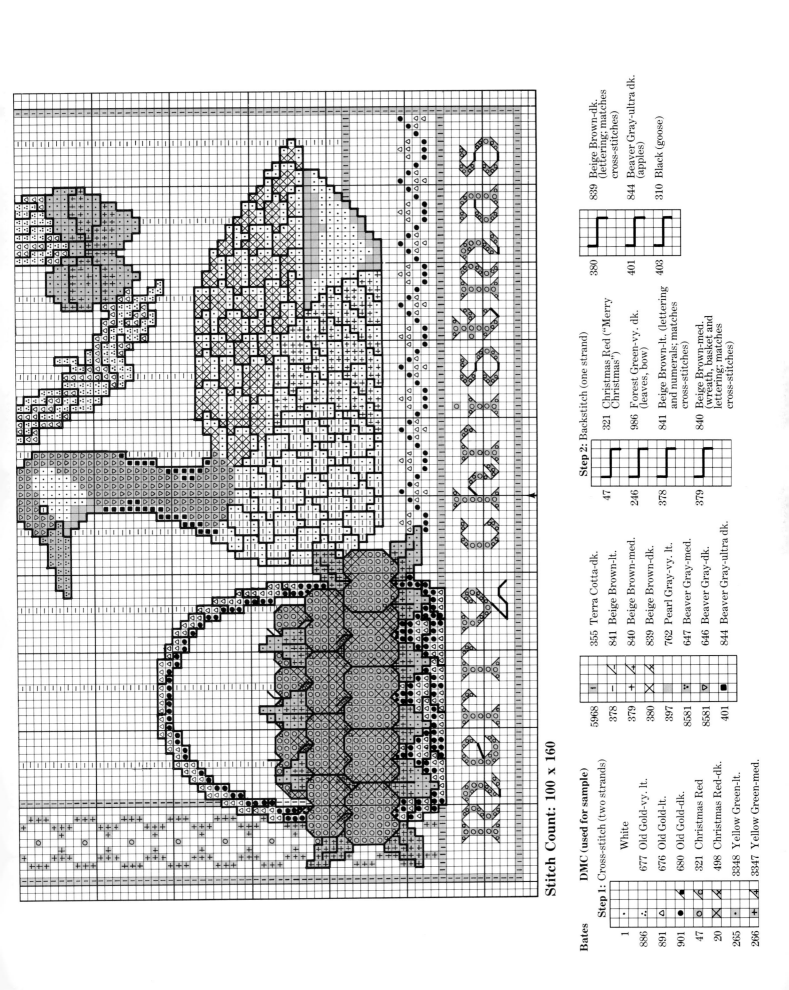

Stitch Count: 100 x 160

Bates   **DMC** (used for sample)

Step 1: Cross-stitch (two strands)

·		−	⁄	+	⁄	
		−		×		
				▢	∴	▽

1		·	White
886		∴	677 Old Gold-vy. lt.
891		▵	676 Old Gold-lt.
901		●	680 Old Gold-dk.
47		○	321 Christmas Red
20		×	498 Christmas Red-dk.
265		·	3348 Yellow Green-lt.
266		+	3347 Yellow Green-med.

5968	355 Terra Cotta-dk.
378	841 Beige Brown-lt.
379	840 Beige Brown-med.
380	839 Beige Brown-dk.
397	762 Pearl Gray-vy. lt.
8581	647 Beaver Gray-med.
8581	646 Beaver Gray-dk.
401	844 Beaver Gray-ultra dk.

380	839 Beige Brown-dk. (lettering; matches cross-stitches)
401	844 Beaver Gray-ultra dk. (apples)
403	310 Black (goose)

Step 2: Backstitch (one strand)

47	321 Christmas Red ("Merry Christmas")
246	986 Forest Green-vy. dk. (leaves, bow)
378	841 Beige Brown-lt. (lettering and numerals; matches cross-stitches)
379	840 Beige Brown-med. (wreath, basket and lettering; matches cross-stitches)

Stitch Count: 100 x 160

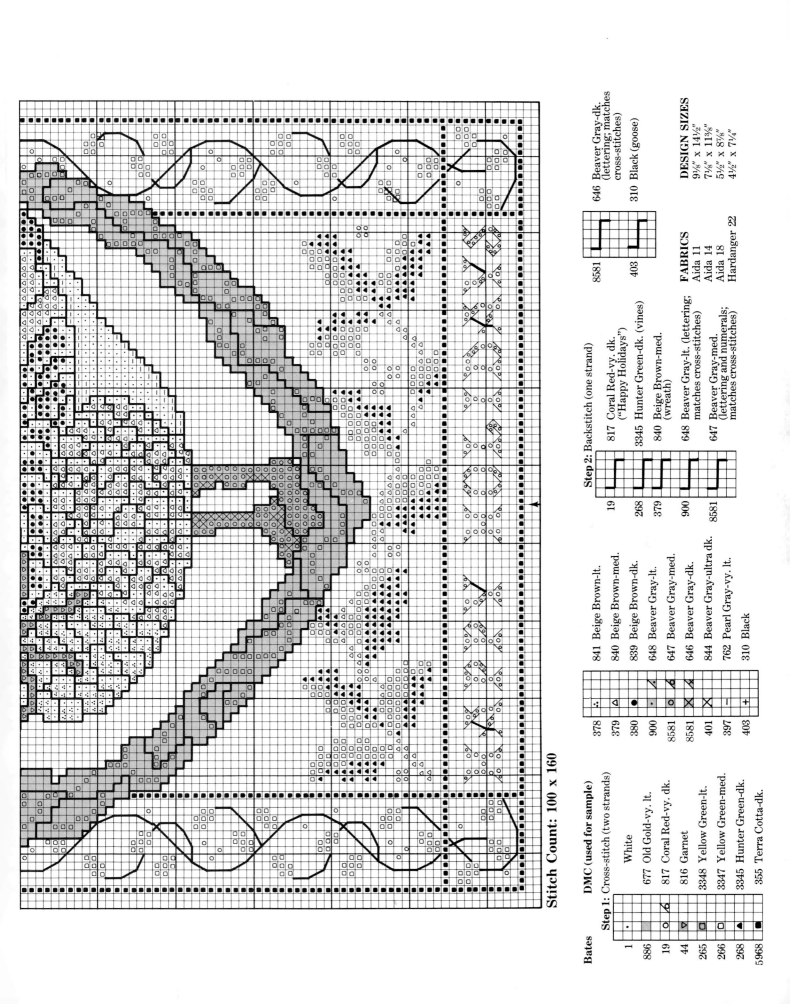

Bates

DMC (used for sample)

Step 1: Cross-stitch (two strands)

1	•	White
886		677 Old Gold-vy. lt.
19		817 Coral Red-vy. dk.
44	▷	816 Garnet
265	□	3348 Yellow Green-lt.
266	☐	3347 Yellow Green-med.
268	◀	3345 Hunter Green-dk.
5968	■	355 Terra Cotta-dk.

378	∴	841 Beige Brown-lt.
379	△	840 Beige Brown-med.
380	●	839 Beige Brown-dk.
900	·	648 Beaver Gray-lt.
8581	○	647 Beaver Gray-med.
8581	✕	646 Beaver Gray-dk.
401	✕	844 Beaver Gray-ultra dk.
397	–	762 Pearl Gray-vy. lt.
403	+	310 Black

8581		646 Beaver Gray-dk. (lettering; matches cross-stitches)
403		310 Black (goose)

Step 2: Backstitch (one strand)

19		817 Coral Red-vy. dk. ("Happy Holidays")
268		3345 Hunter Green-dk. (vines)
379		840 Beige Brown-med. (wreath)
900		648 Beaver Gray-lt. (lettering; matches cross-stitches)
8581		647 Beaver Gray-med. (lettering and numerals; matches cross-stitches)

DESIGN SIZES

9⅛" x 14½"
7⅞" x 11⅜"
5½" x 8⅞"
4½" x 7¼"

FABRICS

Aida 11
Aida 14
Aida 18
Hardanger 22

Angel Sweatshirt

SAMPLE

Stitched on a purchased white sweatshirt using Waste Canvas 14, finished design size is 4⅛" x 4⅝".

Bates			DMC (used for sample)	
Step 1: Cross-stitch (two strands)				
1	−	◿		White
8	·	◿	353	Peach Flesh
10	○	◿	352	Coral-lt.
46	▮	◿	666	Christmas Red-bright
47	✕	◿	321	Christmas Red
47	■		321	Christmas Red (bead sewn over cross-stitch)
120	·	◿	794	Cornflower Blue-lt.
239	▭		702	Kelly Green
227	∴	◿	701	Christmas Green-lt.
923	●	◤	699	Christmas Green
362		◿	437	Tan-lt.
309	○	◿	435	Brown-vy. lt.
371	△		433	Brown-med.
357	✕	◿	801	Coffee Brown-dk.

Step 2: Backstitch (one strand)

47		321	Christmas Red (in stocking)
357		801	Coffee Brown-dk. (all else)

Step 3: French Knots (one strand)

357	●	801	Coffee Brown-dk.

Step 4: Beadwork (sewn over cross-stitch)

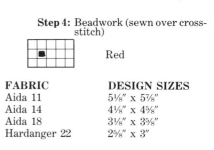

	■	Red

FABRIC	DESIGN SIZES
Aida 11	5⅛" x 5⅛"
Aida 14	4⅛" x 4⅝"
Aida 18	3⅛" x 3⅝"
Hardanger 22	2⅝" x 3"

Stitch Count: 57 x 65

Oh Come All Ye Faithful

SAMPLE

Stitched on white Linda 27 over two threads, the finished design size is 9⅛″ x 5¼″. The fabric was cut 16″ x 12″.

Bates		DMC (used for sample)	
Step 1: Cross-stitch (two strands)			
386	· /	746	Off White
868	−	758	Terra Cotta-lt.
306	o /	725	Topaz
47	X /	304	Christmas Red-med.
70	▲ ▲	3685	Mauve-dk.
167	·	598	Turquoise-lt.
168	X	597	Turquoise
940	/	792	Cornflower Blue-dk.
265	□ /	3348	Yellow Green-lt.
268	● /	937	Avocado Green-med.

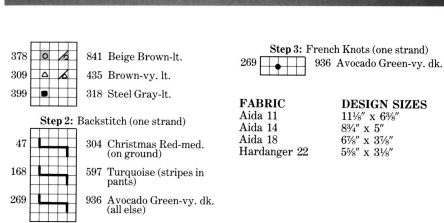

Bates		DMC	
378	o /	841	Beige Brown-lt.
309	△ /	435	Brown-vy. lt.
399	■	318	Steel Gray-lt.

Step 2: Backstitch (one strand)

Bates		DMC	
47		304	Christmas Red-med. (on ground)
168		597	Turquoise (stripes in pants)
269		936	Avocado Green-vy. dk. (all else)

Step 3: French Knots (one strand)

Bates		DMC	
269	●	936	Avocado Green-vy. dk.

FABRIC	DESIGN SIZES
Aida 11	11⅛″ x 6⅜″
Aida 14	8¾″ x 5″
Aida 18	6⅞″ x 3⅞″
Hardanger 22	5⅝″ x 3⅛″

Stitch Count: 123 x 70

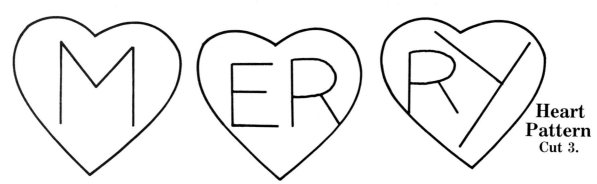

Christmas Tree Wall Hanging

SAMPLES
Stitched on white Aida 18, the moon design is stitched once; remaining designs are stitched three times.

MATERIALS
Completed cross-stitch on white Aida 18: three tree, house, reindeer, and bird designs; one moon design
One 15″ x 18″ piece of dark green pin-dot fabric
⅝ yard of 45″-wide red-and-white striped fabric; matching thread
Small piece of yellow print fabric; matching thread
1⅝ yard of ⅛″-wide white satin ribbon
Thirteen ¼″ dark blue buttons
Small amount of fusing material
One 15″ x 18″ piece of polyester fleece
White acrylic paint, small brush
White thread
One 10″ x 14″ piece of white flannel
Tracing paper for patterns
Dressmakers' pen and chalk

DIRECTIONS
All seams are ¼″.

1. Trace the five pattern pieces for the tree, transferring all information. Also trace the patterns for the star, heart, and scallops.

2. Center the five tree patterns over the corresponding stitched designs and trace around them with a dressmakers' pen. Add ¼″ seam allowances on all sides of the patterns when cutting.

3. From the red fabric, cut one 15″ x 18″ piece for the back of the wall hanging, three hearts, and 1¾″-wide bias strips, piecing as needed to equal 2 yards.

4. From the yellow fabric, cut one star.

5. From the fusing material, cut three hearts and one star.

6. With right sides together, pin the curved edges of one tree, house, reindeer, and bird section to form a vertical row (see photo). Stitch together by hand. Use the remaining sections to make the two additional rows. Stitch the long edges of the three units together by hand or machine. Hand-stitch the moon section to the top of the tree.

7. Using the Aida tree as a pattern, place it over the flannel and cut one tree. Trim away ¼″ on all sides and pin to the wrong side of the Aida tree. Baste the two pieces together by hand.

8. Mark the quilting pattern on the green fabric with the dressmakers' chalk. The vertical grid lines are 1½″ apart. The first horizontal line is ¾″ from the top edge of the fabric, with the remaining lines 1½″ apart. Trace the star, with the point ¼″ to the right of the center of the green fabric and 1½″ from the top edge.

9. Center the Aida tree ⅛″ below the star and baste to the green fabric. Fold the edges of the tree under ¼″ and slipstitch in place.

10. With the dressmakers' chalk, trace the scallop quilting pattern under the tree.

11. Center and fuse three hearts, ⅛″ apart, below the scallops. Position the star and fuse in place. Machine satin-stitch the outside edges of the hearts and the star.

12. Mark "Merry" with a dressmakers' pen or chalk. Machine satin-stitch the letters on the hearts with white thread.

13. Dilute a small amount of white paint. Paint the trunk to within ⅛″ of the hearts, filling two whole grid squares (see photo).

14. Place the red backing fabric, wrong side up, on a flat surface. Layer the fleece and the front of the wall hanging, right side up, over the back. Baste the three layers together.

15. With white thread, quilt by hand around the tree, star, hearts, scallops, and on all grid lines.

16. Sew the blue buttons under the center section of the tree, following the scallop quilting lines (see photo).

17. Stitch the right sides of the binding and wall hanging together with a ¼″ seam, allowing extra fullness at the corners. Fold under ¼″ of opposite edge of bias strip, and then fold to the back. Slipstitch in place.

continued . . .

Moon: The finished design size is 2⅝″ x 1½″. Fabric was cut 6″ x 6″.

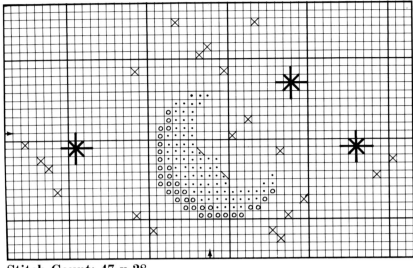

Stitch Count: 47 x 28

Bates		DMC (used for sample)
Step 1: Cross-stitch (two strands)		
297		743 Yellow-med.
303		742 Tangerine-lt.
Step 2: Backstitch (one strand)		
297		743 Yellow-med.
Step 3: Beadwork		
		Light Blue

FABRICS	DESIGN SIZES
Aida 11	4¼″ x 2½″
Aida 14	3⅜″ x 2″
Hardanger 22	2⅛″ x 1¼″

Birds: The finished design size is 1¼″ x 1½″. Fabric was cut 6″ x 6″.

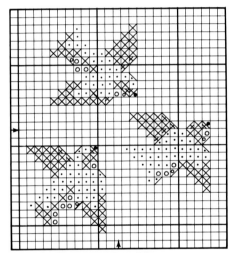

Stitch Count: 23 x 26

Bates		DMC (used for sample)
Step 1: Cross-stitch (two strands)		
303		742 Tangerine-lt.
35		891 Carnation-dk.
130		809 Delft
131		798 Delft-dk.

FABRICS	DESIGN SIZES
Aida 11	2⅛″ x 2⅜″
Aida 14	1⅝″ x 1⅞″
Hardanger 22	1″ x 1⅛″

Reindeer: Finished design size is 2⅛″ x 1⅛″. Fabric was cut 6″ x 6″.

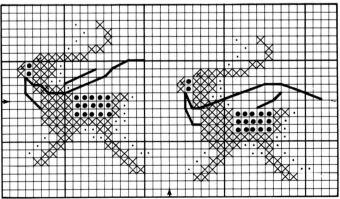

Stitch Count: 38 x 20

Bates		DMC (used for sample)
Step 1: Cross-stitch (two strands)		
35		891 Carnation-dk.
351		400 Mahogany-dk.
352		300 Mahogany-vy. dk.
Step 2: Backstitch (one strand)		
35		891 Carnation-dk.

FABRICS	DESIGN SIZES
Aida 11	3½″ x 1¾″
Aida 14	2¾″ x 1⅜″
Hardanger 22	1¾″ x ⅞″

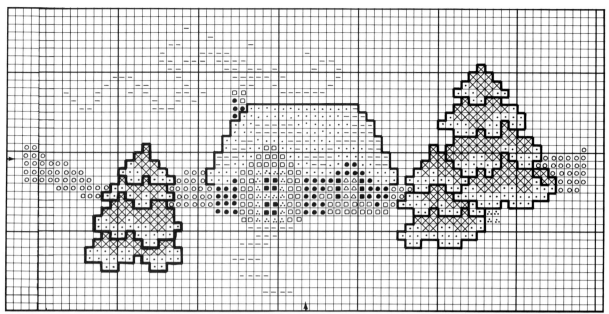

Stitch Count: 71 x 34

House: The finished design size is 4″ x 1⅞″. The fabric was cut 6″ x 6″.

Bates		DMC (used for sample)
Step 1: Cross-stitch (two strands)		
1	·	White
303	△	742 Tangerine-lt.
35	□	891 Carnation-dk.
47	●	321 Christmas Red
128	○	800 Delft-pale
228	✕	910 Emerald Green-dk.
351	∴	400 Mahogany-dk.
352	■	300 Mahogany-vy. dk.
397	–	762 Pearl Gray-vy. lt.

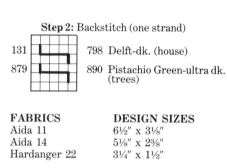

		Step 2: Backstitch (one strand)	
131		798 Delft-dk. (house)	
879		890 Pistachio Green-ultra dk. (trees)	

FABRICS	DESIGN SIZES
Aida 11	6½″ x 3⅛″
Aida 14	5⅛″ x 2⅜″
Hardanger 22	3¼″ x 1½″

Trees: The finished design size is 4⅞″ x 1⅝″. Fabric was cut 7″ x 6″.

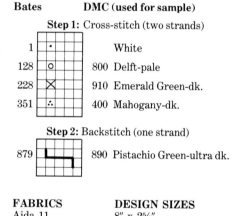

Bates		DMC (used for sample)
Step 1: Cross-stitch (two strands)		
1	·	White
128	○	800 Delft-pale
228	✕	910 Emerald Green-dk.
351	∴	400 Mahogany-dk.

		Step 2: Backstitch (one strand)	
879		890 Pistachio Green-ultra dk.	

FABRICS	DESIGN SIZES
Aida 11	8″ x 2⅝″
Aida 14	6¼″ x 2⅛″
Hardanger 22	4″ x 1⅜″

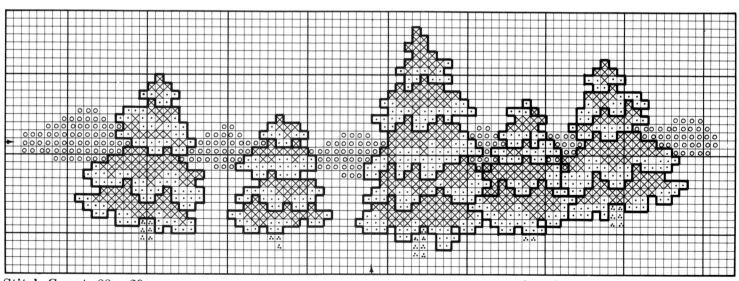

Stitch Count: 88 x 29

continued . . .

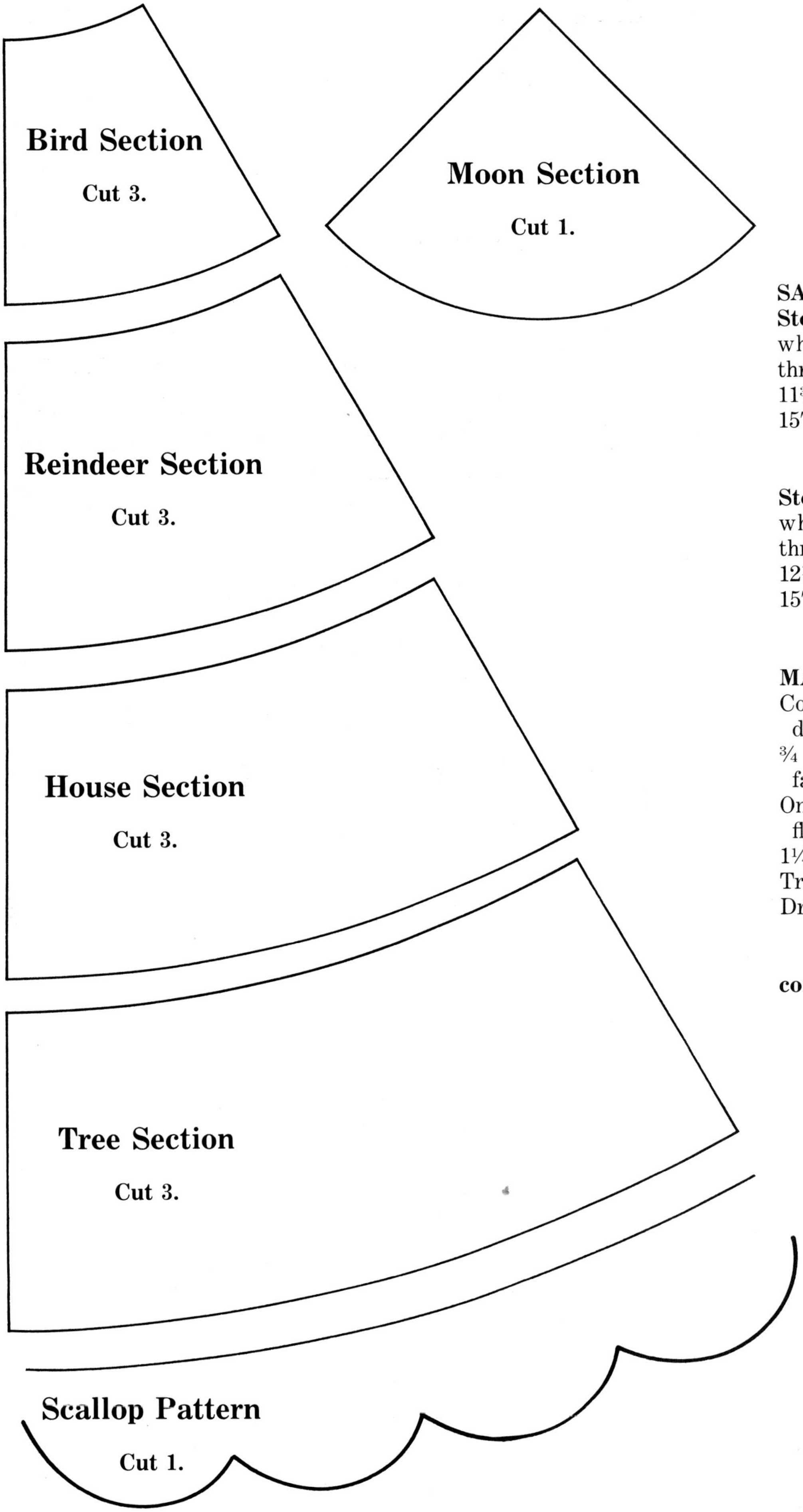

Bird Section

Cut 3.

Moon Section

Cut 1.

Angel Stockings

SAMPLES
Stocking with Sheep: Stitched on white Hardanger 22 over two threads, the finished design size is 11¾″ x 14½″. The fabric was cut 15″ x 18″.

Stocking with Sleigh: Stitched on white Hardanger 22 over two threads, the finished design size is 12¼″ x 13¾″. The fabric was cut 15″ x 18″.

Reindeer Section

Cut 3.

MATERIALS (for one stocking)
Completed cross-stitch on Hardanger 22 over two threads
¾ yard of 45″-wide powder blue fabric; matching thread
One 13″ x 18″ piece of polyester fleece
1¼ yards of medium cording
Tracing paper for pattern
Dressmakers' pen

House Section

Cut 3.

continued . . .

Tree Section

Cut 3.

Scallop Pattern

Cut 1.

Star Pattern

Cut 1.

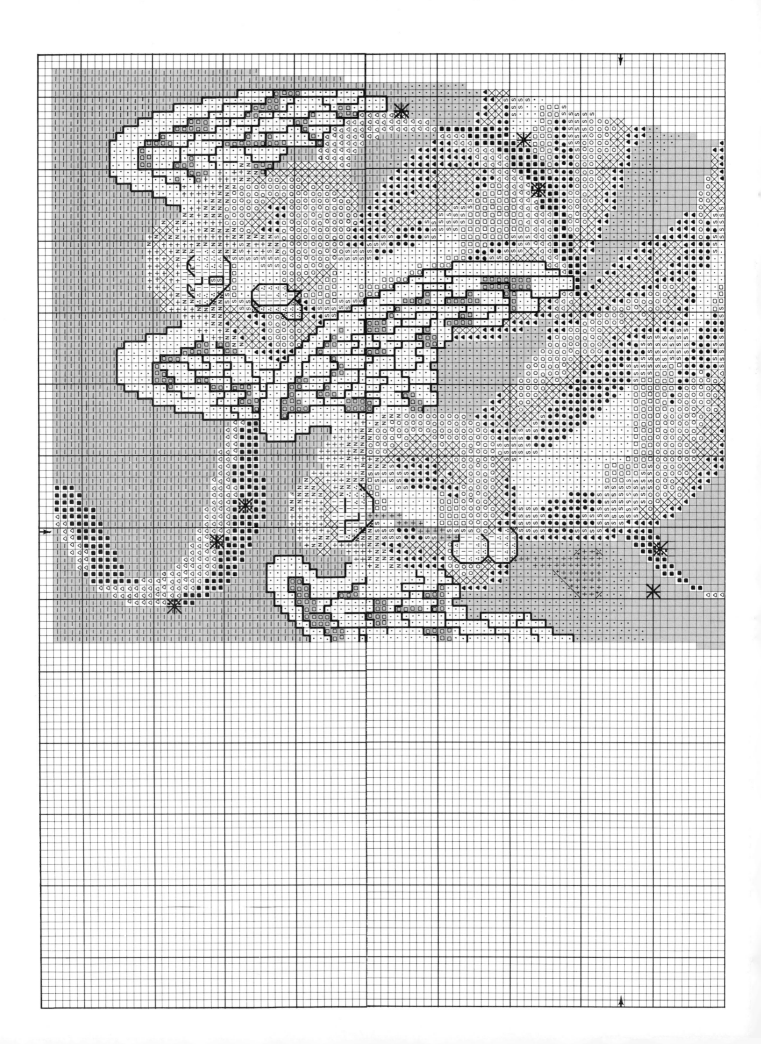

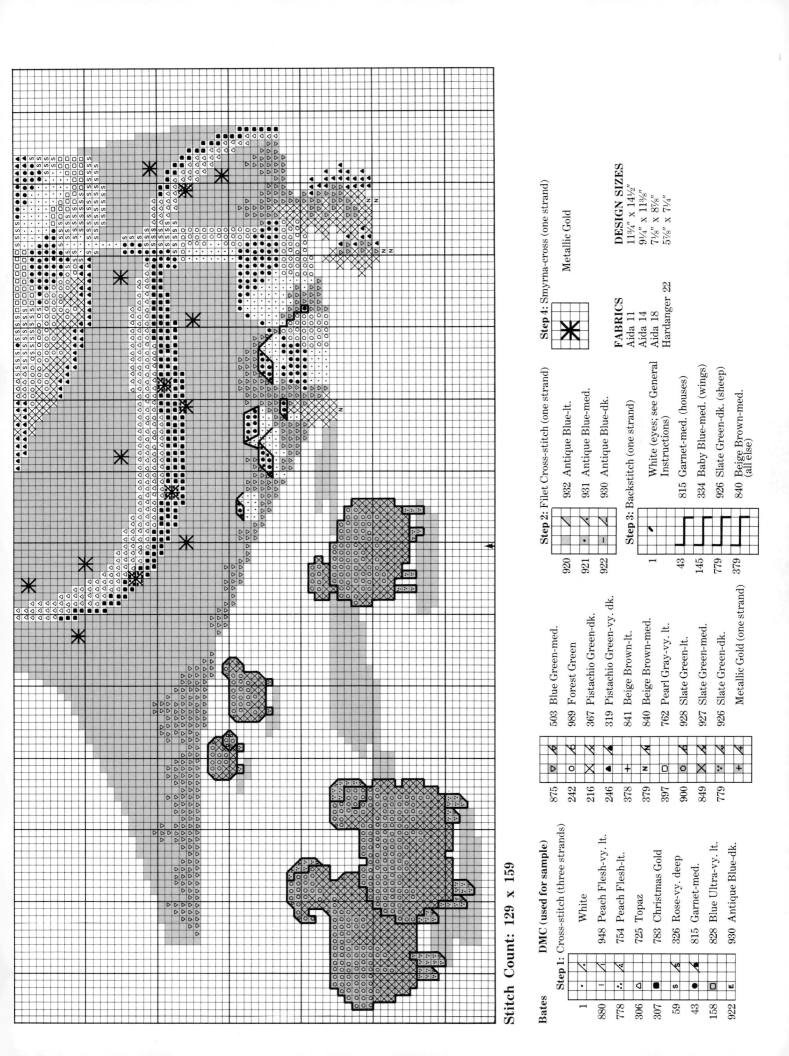

Stitch Count: 129 x 159

Bates **DMC (used for sample)**

Step 1: Cross-stitch (three strands)

1	·	White
880	l	948 Peach Flesh-vy. lt.
778	⠇ ⠄	754 Peach Flesh-lt.
306	△	725 Topaz
307	■	783 Christmas Gold
59	s	326 Rose-vy. deep
43	●	815 Garnet-med.
158	□	828 Blue Ultra-vy. lt.
922	E	930 Antique Blue-dk.

875	▷	503 Blue Green-med.
242	○	989 Forest Green
216	✕	367 Pistachio Green-dk.
246	◢	319 Pistachio Green-vy. dk.
378	+	841 Beige Brown-lt.
379	N	840 Beige Brown-med.
397	□	762 Pearl Gray-vy. lt.
900	○	928 Slate Green-lt.
849	✕	927 Slate Green-med.
779	⠢	926 Slate Green-dk.
	+	Metallic Gold (one strand)

Step 2: Filet Cross-stitch (one strand)

920		932 Antique Blue-lt.
921	·	931 Antique Blue-med.
922	−	930 Antique Blue-dk.

Step 3: Backstitch (one strand)

1	White (eyes; see General Instructions)
43	815 Garnet-med. (houses)
145	334 Baby Blue-med. (wings)
779	926 Slate Green-dk. (sheep)
379	840 Beige Brown-med. (all else)

Step 4: Smyrna-cross (one strand)

Metallic Gold

FABRICS   **DESIGN SIZES**
Aida 11   11¾" x 14½"
Aida 14   9¼" x 11⅜"
Aida 18   7⅛" x 8⅞"
Hardanger 22   5⅝" x 7¼"

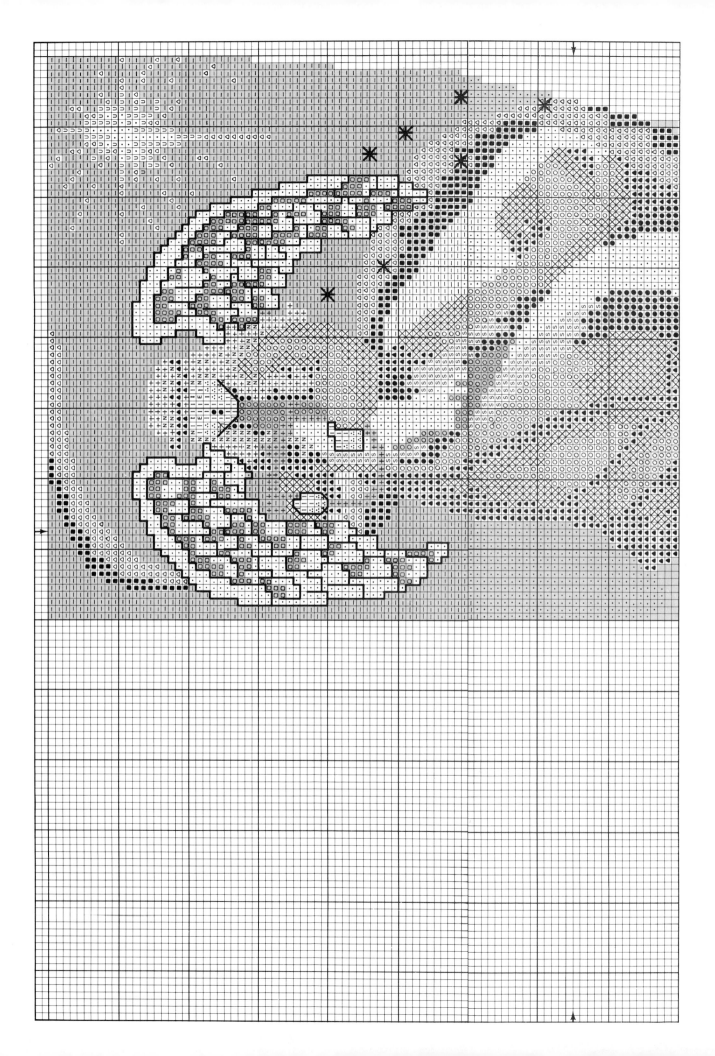

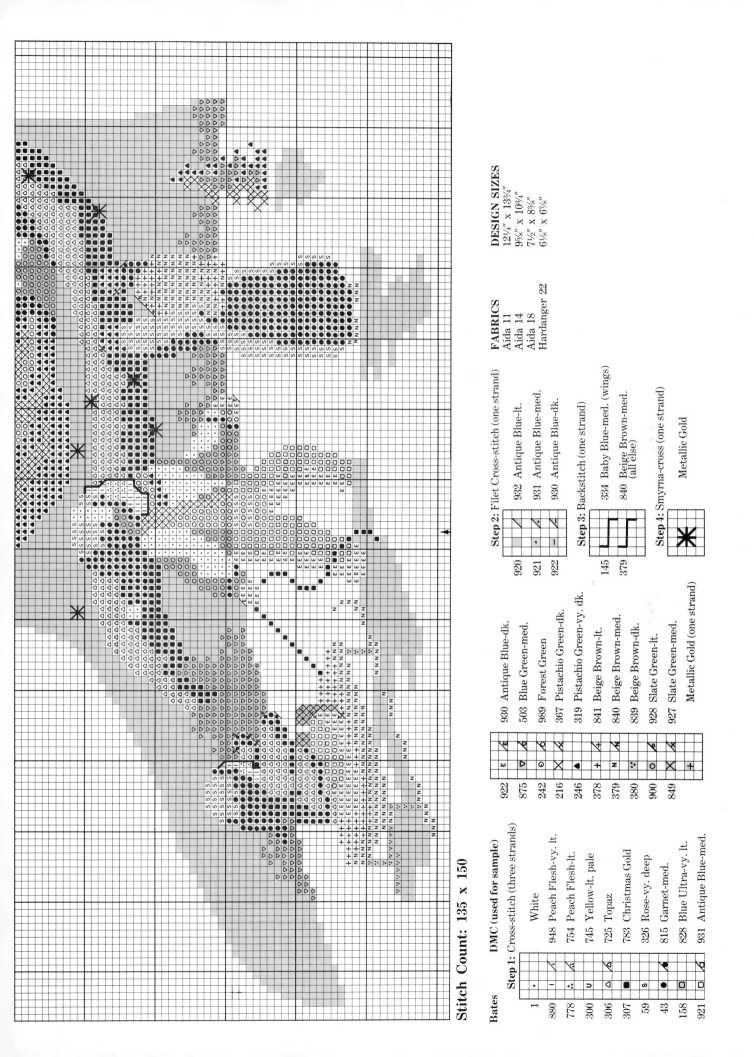

Stitch Count: 135 x 150

Bates **DMC (used for sample)**

Step 1: Cross-stitch (three strands)

1	·	White
880	⁄	948 Peach Flesh-vy. lt.
778	⁞	754 Peach Flesh-lt.
300	∪	745 Yellow-lt. pale
306	△	725 Topaz
307	■	783 Christmas Gold
59	s	326 Rose-vy. deep
43	●	815 Garnet-med.
158	▢	828 Blue Ultra-vy. lt.
921	◻	931 Antique Blue-med.

922	E	930 Antique Blue-dk.
875	▷	503 Blue Green-med.
242	◑	989 Forest Green
216	☒	367 Pistachio Green-dk.
246	◀	319 Pistachio Green-vy. dk.
378	+	841 Beige Brown-lt.
379	N	840 Beige Brown-med.
380	∴	839 Beige Brown-dk.
900	○	928 Slate Green-lt.
849	⊠	927 Slate Green-med.
	+	Metallic Gold (one strand)

Step 2: Filet Cross-stitch (one strand)

920	◹	932 Antique Blue-lt.
921	·	931 Antique Blue-med.
922	—	930 Antique Blue-dk.

Step 3: Backstitch (one strand)

145	334 Baby Blue-med. (wings)
379	840 Beige Brown-med. (all else)

Step 4: Smyrna-cross (one strand)

✳ Metallic Gold

FABRICS

Aida 11
Aida 14
Aida 18
Hardanger 22

DESIGN SIZES

12¼" x 13¾"
9⅝" x 10¾"
7½" x 8⅜"
6⅛" x 6⅞"

Each square = 1 inch.

DIRECTIONS
All seams are ¼″.

1. Enlarge and trace the pattern for the stocking.

2. For the stocking front, align the top edge of the pattern with the top edge of the stitched design. The toe and lower edge may extend several inches beyond the design. Add ¼″ seam allowances as you cut.

3. From the blue fabric, cut one stocking piece for the back, two stocking pieces for the lining, and one 2″ x 4″ piece for the loop. Cut 1¼″-wide bias strips, piecing as needed, to equal 45″. Cover the cording (see General Instructions).

4. From the polyester fleece, cut one stocking piece.

5. With raw edges aligned, stitch the cording to the right side of the stocking front. Pin the fleece to the wrong side of the stocking front and baste. With right sides of the stocking front and back together, stitch on the stitching line of the cording. Trim seams and clip curves. Turn right side out.

6. Stitch the two lining pieces, right sides together, leaving a 4″ opening in the seam above the heel. Trim seams and clip curves. Fold the loop piece in half, to measure 1″ x 4″, and stitch along the 4″ side. Trim and turn. Fold the loop in half. Aligning raw edges, pin the loop to the top left edge of the stocking back.

7. With right sides together, slide the lining over the Hardanger stocking, matching seams at the top edge. Stitch the top edge, securing the loop in the seam. Turn the stocking through the opening. Slipstitch the opening closed.

8. Tuck the lining inside the stocking, allowing ¼″ of the lining to show along the top edge. By hand, secure the lining to the seam allowance.

Father Frost

SAMPLE
Stitched on white Belfast Linen 32 over two threads, the finished design size is 8¼" x 10¾". The fabric was cut 14" x 17".

continued . . .

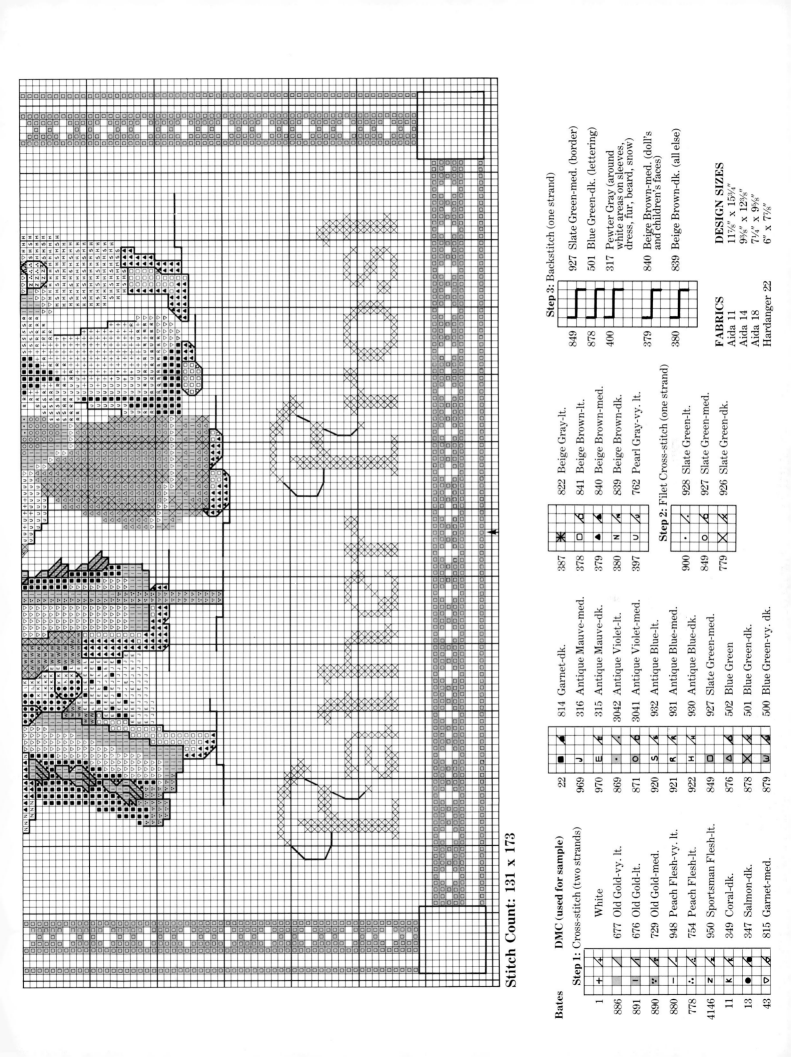

Stitch Count: 131 x 173

Step 1: Cross-stitch (two strands)

Bates	DMC (used for sample)
1	White
886	677 Old Gold-vy. lt.
891	676 Old Gold-lt.
890	729 Old Gold-med.
880	948 Peach Flesh-vy. lt.
778	754 Peach Flesh-lt.
4146	950 Sportsman Flesh-lt.
11	349 Coral-dk.
13	347 Salmon-dk.
43	815 Garnet-med.

22	814 Garnet-dk.
969	316 Antique Mauve-med.
970	315 Antique Mauve-dk.
869	3042 Antique Violet-lt.
871	3041 Antique Violet-med.
920	932 Antique Blue-lt.
921	931 Antique Blue-med.
922	930 Antique Blue-dk.
849	927 Slate Green-med.
876	502 Blue Green
878	501 Blue Green-dk.
879	500 Blue Green-vy. dk.

387	822 Beige Gray-lt.
378	841 Beige Brown-lt.
379	840 Beige Brown-med.
380	839 Beige Brown-dk.
397	762 Pearl Gray-vy. lt.

Step 2: Filet Cross-stitch (one strand)

900	928 Slate Green-lt.
849	927 Slate Green-med.
779	926 Slate Green-dk.

Step 3: Backstitch (one strand)

849	927 Slate Green-med. (border)
878	501 Blue Green-dk. (lettering)
400	317 Pewter Gray (around white areas on sleeves, dress, fur, beard, snow)
379	840 Beige Brown-med. (doll's and children's faces)
380	839 Beige Brown-dk. (all else)

DESIGN SIZES
11⅞" x 15¾"
9⅜" x 12⅜"
7¼" x 9⅝"
6" x 7⅞"

FABRICS
Aida 11
Aida 14
Aida 18
Hardanger 22

Hark the Herald Angels Sing

SAMPLE
Stitched on Glenshee Egyptian Cotton 26 over two threads, the finished design size is 10¾″ x 5¼″. The fabric was cut 17″ x 11″.

Bates			DMC	(used for sample)
		Step 1:	Cross-stitch (two strands)	
887	·	⁄	3046	Yellow Beige-med.
868	+	⁄	758	Terra Cotta-lt.
5975	◊	⁄	356	Terra Cotta-med.
5968	–	⁄	355	Terra Cotta-dk.
101	●		550	Violet-vy. dk.
159	I		827	Blue-vy. lt.
920	◭		932	Antique Blue-lt.
160	·	⁄	813	Blue-lt.
161	○	⁄	826	Blue-med.
266	✕	⁄	3347	Yellow Green-med.
257	▽		3346	Hunter Green
210		⁄	562	Jade-med.
212	●	⁄	561	Jade-vy. dk.
362	□		437	Tan-lt.
363	▼		436	Tan
378	⁚	⁄	841	Beige Brown-lt.
397	⁖		762	Pearl Gray-vy. lt.
401	▢		413	Pewter Gray-dk.

Step 2: Filet Cross-stitch (one strand)

887	✕	⁄	3046	Yellow Beige-med.

Step 3: Backstitch (one strand)

382		3371	Black Brown

Step 4: French Knot (one strand)

382	●	3371	Black Brown

FABRICS
FABRICS	DESIGN SIZES
Aida 11	12⅝″ x 6⅛″
Aida 14	9⅞″ x 4⅞″
Aida 18	7¾″ x 3¾″
Hardanger 22	6⅜″ x 3⅛″

138

Stitch Count: 139 x 68

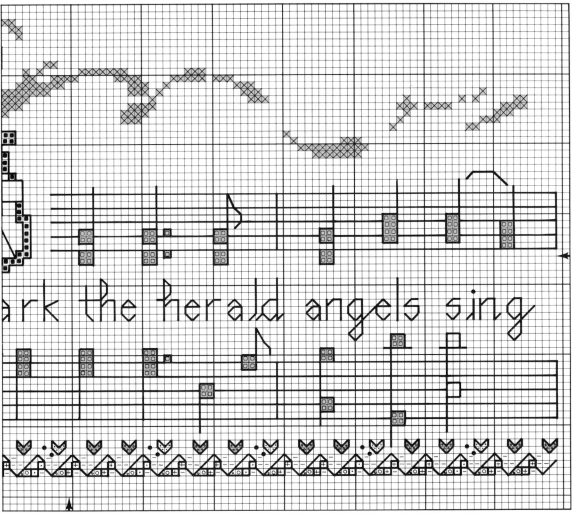

I'm Yours Firever

SAMPLE

Stitched on muslin, using Waste Canvas 14 over two sets of threads, the finished design size is 1⅞" x 2¼". Cut waste canvas 3½" x 3½". (See page 14 for specific instructions for making the quilt.)

FABRICS	DESIGN SIZES
Aida 11	1⅛" x 1½"
Aida 14	⅞" x 1⅛"
Aida 18	¾" x ⅞"
Hardanger 22	⅝" x ¾"

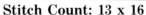

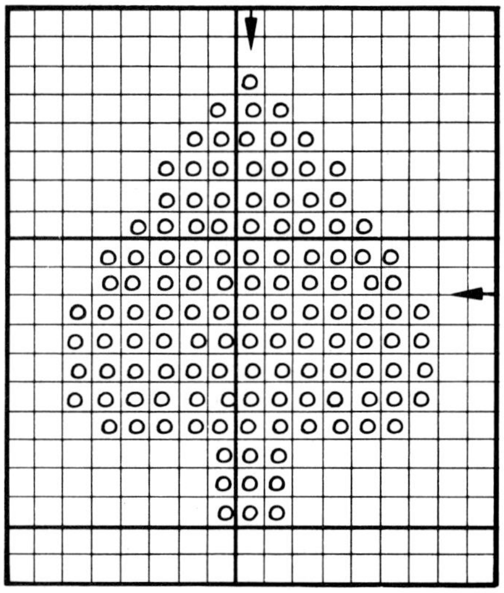

Stitch Count: 13 x 16

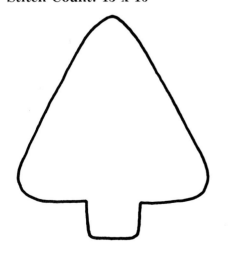

I'M

YOURS

FIREVER

General Instructions

SEWING HINTS

Bias Strips: Bias strips are used for ruffles, binding, or cording. To cut bias, fold the fabric at a 45° angle to the grain of the fabric and crease. Cut on the crease. Cut additional strips the width indicated in instructions and parallel to the first cutting line. The ends of the bias strips should be on the grain of fabric. Place the right sides of the ends together and stitch with a ¼″ seam (Diagram A). Continue to piece the strips until they are the length indicated in instructions.

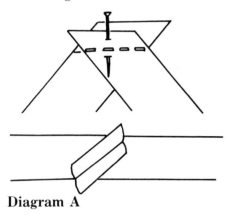

Diagram A

Cording (also called welting or piping): Piece bias strips together to equal the length needed for cording. Place the cord in the center of the wrong side of the strip and fold the fabric over it. Using a zipper foot, stitch close to the cord through both layers of fabric (Diagram B). Trim the seam allowance ¼″ from the stitching line.

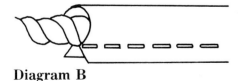

Diagram B

Clipping Seams: Clipping seam allowances is necessary on all curves and points and on most corners, so that the finished seam will lie flat. Clip into the seam allowance at even intervals, ¼″ to ½″ apart, being careful not to cut through the stitching (Diagram C).

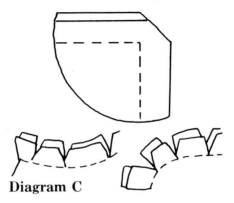

Diagram C

CROSS-STITCH

Fabrics: Most fabrics used in this book are even-weave fabrics made especially for cross-stitch and are available in needlework departments or shops. If you cannot find the fabrics in your area, refer to Suppliers, page 143. Fabrics used for the models in the photographs are identified in the sample information by color, name, and thread count per inch.

Finished Design Size: To determine the finished size of a design, divide the stitch count by the number of threads per inch in the fabric. When designs are stitched over two threads, divide the stitch count by half of the threads per inch.

Needles: Use a blunt tapestry needle that slips easily through the holes and does not pierce the fabric. With fabric that has eleven or fewer threads per inch, use needle size 24; with fourteen threads per inch, use needle size 24 or 26; with eighteen threads or more per inch, use needle size 26.

Preparing Fabric: Cut the fabric 3″ larger on all sides than the finished design size, or cut as indicated in the sample information. To keep the fabric from fraying, whipstitch or machine-zigzag the raw edges.

Hoop or Frame: Select a hoop or stretcher bars large enough to hold the entire design. Place the screw or the clamp of the hoop in a 10 o'clock position (or 2 o'clock, if you are left-handed) to keep it from catching the thread.

Floss: Cut the floss into 18″ lengths. For best coverage, run the floss over a damp sponge and separate all six strands. Put back together the number of strands recommended for use in the sample information. If the floss becomes twisted while stitching, drop the needle and allow the floss to unwind. The floss will cover best when lying flat.

Centering Design: Find the center of the fabric by folding it from top to bottom and again from left to right. Place a pin in the point of the fold to mark the center. Locate the center of the graph by following the vertical and horizontal arrows. Begin stitching at the center point of the graph and fabric. Each square on the graph represents one complete cross-stitch. Unless indicated otherwise in the sample information, each stitch is over one unit of thread.

Securing Floss: Never knot floss unless working on clothing. Hold 1″ of floss behind the fabric and secure the floss with the first few stitches. To secure the floss when finishing, run it under four or more stitches on the back of the design.

Backstitching: Complete all cross-stitches before working backstitches or accent stitches. When backstitching, use the number of strands indicated in the code or one strand fewer than was used for cross-stitching.

Stitching Method: For a smooth stitch, use a push-and-pull method. Push the needle straight down and completely through the fabric before pulling it up.

Carrying Floss: Do not carry floss more than ½″ between stitched areas because loose threads, especially dark ones, will show through the fabric. Run the floss under worked stitches on the back when possible.

Cleaning Completed Work: After making sure fabric and floss are colorfast, briefly soak the completed work in cold water. If it is soiled, wash it gently in mild soap. Roll the work in a towel to remove excess water; do not wring. Place the work face down on a dry lightweight towel and press it with a warm iron until it is dry.

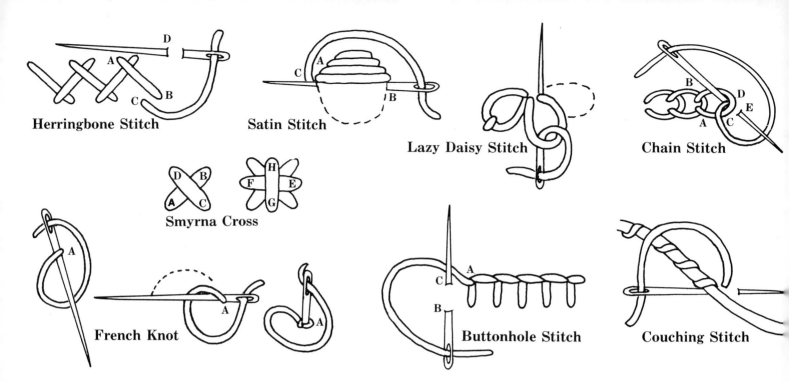

Herringbone Stitch

Satin Stitch

Lazy Daisy Stitch

Chain Stitch

Smyrna Cross

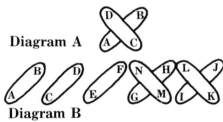

French Knot

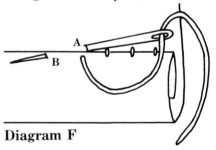

Buttonhole Stitch

Couching Stitch

STITCHES

Cross-Stitch: Bring the needle and thread up at A, down at B, up at C, and down again at D (Diagram A). For rows, stitch all the way across so that the floss is angled from the lower left to the upper right; then return (Diagram B). *All the stitches should lie in the same direction.*

Diagram A

Diagram B

Filet Cross-Stitch: Filet cross-stitch is simply cross-stitch that uses only one strand of embroidery floss. It is usually used for the background of a design, while the design itself is cross-stitched with enough strands to cover the fabric. When complete, the background resembles a delicate net (see Jesus and the Children, page 47).

Filet cross-stitch is a modern interpretation of a lace-making technique called "filet brode." Designs having a definite positive and negative pattern work best (see A Barnful of Pets, page 59). The number of strands to use for cross-stitch and filet cross-stitch are designated in the code for each design.

Beadwork: With one strand of embroidery floss, attach beads to fabric with a half-cross, lower left to upper right. Secure the beads by returning the thread through the beads, lower right to upper left. Complete an entire row of half-crosses before returning to secure all the beads. See Suppliers for a source of beads used for the projects throughout the book.

Half-Cross: Indicated on the graph by a slanted line with the color symbol beside it; make the longer stitch in the direction of the slanted line. The stitch actually fits three-fourths of the area (Diagram C). Bring the needle and thread up at A and down at B, up at C and down at D. In cases where two colors meet, the graph will indicate how both colors make up the completed stitch (Diagram D).

Diagram C

Diagram D

Backstitch: Work from left to right with one strand of floss (unless indicated otherwise in the code). Bring needle and thread up at A, down at B, and up again at C. Going back down at A, continue to stitch in this manner (Diagram E).

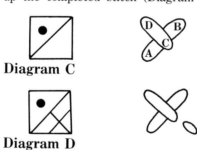

Diagram E

Slipstitch: Working from right to left, insert needle at A, slide it through the folded edge of the fabric for about ⅛" to ¼", and bring it out at B (Diagram F). Directly below B, take a small stitch through the second piece of fabric.

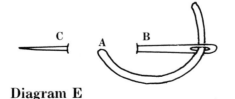

Diagram F

Stitching Eyes on People: Complete the cross-stitch in the background color according to the code. Then, using one strand of white floss, stitch a quarter-stitch over the cross-stitch at the angle shown on the graph.

WORKING WITH WASTE CANVAS

Cut the waste canvas 1" larger on all sides than the finished design size. Baste the waste canvas to the fabric or paper to be stitched. Complete the stitching; each stitch is over one unit (two threads), except on the little quilts. When stitching is complete, use a spray bottle to dampen the stitched area with cold water. Pull the waste canvas threads out one at a time with tweezers. It is easier to pull all the threads running in one direction first; then pull out the opposite threads. Allow the stitching to dry; then place face down on a towel and iron.

Jacket Motifs

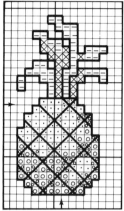

Stitch Count: 12 x 24

Bates		DMC (used for sample)
Step 1: Cross-stitch (two strands)		
891	·	676 Old Gold-lt.
901	o	680 Old Gold-dk.
215	–	368 Pistachio Green-lt.
216	X	367 Pistachio Green-dk.
Step 2: Backstitch (one strand)		
382		3371 Black Brown

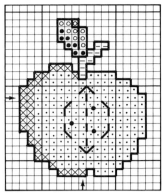

Stitch Count: 17 x 21

Bates		DMC (used for sample)
Step 1: Cross-stitch (two strands)		
386	·	746 Off White
47	X	304 Christmas Red-med.
215	o	368 Pistachio Green-lt.
216	●	367 Pistachio Green-dk.
308	–	976 Golden Brown-med.
Step 2: Backstitch (one strand)		
47		304 Christmas Red-med. (right edge of apple)
382		3371 Black Brown (stem, leaf, core, outline)
Step 3: French Knots (one strand)		
382	●	3371 Black Brown

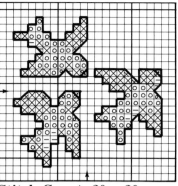

Stitch Count: 20 x 20

Bates		DMC (used for sample)
Step 1: Cross-stitch (two strands)		
891	/	676 Old Gold-lt.
47	– /	304 Christmas Red-med.
159	o /	827 Blue-vy. lt.
161	X /	826 Blue-med.
Step 2: Backstitch (one strand)		
382		3371 Black Brown

Suppliers

If you are unable to locate a particular item in your local needlework store, write to the following manufacturers for a list of distributors in your area.

Linen 26—Wichelt Imports, Inc., Rural Route 1, Stoddard, WI 54658.

Linaida—Charles Craft, P.O. Box 1049, Laurinburg, NC 28352.

Other fabrics—Joan Toggitt, 246 Fifth Ave., New York, NY 10001.

Metallic thread—Kreinik Manufacturing, P.O. Box 1966, Parkersburg, WV 26101.

Beads—MPR Associates, P.O. Box 7343, High Point, NC 27264. The following colors were used for the projects in this book.

128T-Yellow	332-Emerald
145T-Pink	367-Garnet
146T-Light Blue	423-Tangerine
165T-Christmas Red	431-Jade Green
167T-Christmas Green	525K-Light Green
168T-Sapphire	534-Lilac
252T-Iris	968K-Red

Ribbon—C. M. Offray & Son, Route 24, Box 601, Chester, NJ 07930-0601.

Retail orders—for towels and tote bags write Chapelle Designers, P.O. 9252, Newgate Station, Ogden, UT 84409. For all other items, write to Shepherd's Bush, 220 24th Street, Ogden, UT 84401.

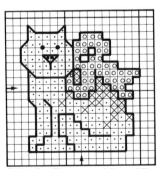

Stitch Count: 16 x 17

Bates		DMC (used for sample)
Step 1: Cross-stitch (two strands)		
891	· /	676 Old Gold-lt.
161	o /	826 Blue-med.
363	X	436 Tan
382	/	3371 Black Brown
Step 2: Backstitch (one strand)		
382		3371 Black Brown
Step 3: French Knots (one strand)		
382	●	3371 Black Brown

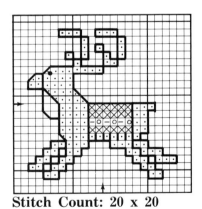

Stitch Count: 20 x 20

Bates		DMC (used for sample)
Step 1: Cross-stitch (two strands)		
891	o	676 Old Gold-lt.
47	X	304 Christmas Red-med.
216	–	367 Pistachio Green-dk.
379	· /	840 Beige Brown-med.
Step 2: Backstitch (one strand)		
47		304 Christmas Red-med. (reins, blanket; see jacket)
382		3371 Black Brown (reindeer)
Step 3: French Knots (one strand)		
382	●	3371 Black Brown